House of Commons

International Development Committee

Conflict and Development: Peacebuilding and Post–conflict Reconstruction

Sixth Report of Session 2005–06

Volume I

Report, together with formal minutes

*Ordered by The House of Commons
to be printed 17 October 2006*

HC 923-I
Published on 25 October 2006
by authority of the House of Commons
London: The Stationery Office Limited
£13.50

International Development Committee

The International Development Committee is appointed by the House of Commons to examine the expenditure, administration, and policy of the Department for International Development and its associated public bodies.

Current membership

Malcolm Bruce MP (*Liberal Democrat, Gordon*) (Chairman)
John Barrett MP (*Liberal Democrat, Edinburgh West*)
John Battle MP (*Labour, Leeds West*)
Hugh Bayley MP (*Labour, City of York*)
John Bercow MP (*Conservative, Buckingham*)
Richard Burden MP (*Labour, Birmingham Northfield*)
Mr Quentin Davies MP (*Conservative, Grantham and Stamford*)
James Duddridge MP *(Conservative, Rochford and Southend East)*
Ann McKechin MP (*Labour, Glasgow North*)
Joan Ruddock MP (*Labour, Lewisham Deptford*)
Mr Marsha Singh MP (*Labour, Bradford West*)

Mr Jeremy Hunt MP (*Conservative, South West Surrey*) was also a member of the Committee during this inquiry.

Powers

The Committee is one of the departmental select committees, the powers of which are set out in House of Commons Standing Orders, principally in SO No 152. These are available on the Internet via www.parliament.uk.

Publications

The Reports and evidence of the Committee are published by The Stationery Office by Order of the House. All publications of the Committee (including press notices) are on the Internet at www.parliament.uk/indcom

Committee staff

The staff of the Committee are Carol Oxborough (Clerk), Hannah Weston, Matthew Hedges (Second Clerks), Anna Dickson (Committee Specialist), Chlöe Challender (Committee Specialist), Katie Phelan (Committee Assistant), Jennifer Steele (Secretary) and Louise Glen (Senior Office Clerk).

Contacts

All correspondence should be addressed to the Clerk of the International Development Committee, House of Commons, 7 Millbank, London SW1P 3JA. The telephone number for general enquiries is 020 7219 1223; the Committee's email address is indcom@parliament.uk

Footnotes

In the footnotes of this Report, references to oral evidence are indicated by 'Q' followed by the question number. References to written evidence are indicated by the page number as in 'Ev 12'.

Contents

Summary

Violent conflict has killed and displaced more people in Africa than in any other continent in recent decades according to the Commission for Africa. This severely challenges the achievement of the Millennium Development Goals in these countries.

Conflicts are also costly. It is estimated that the cost of each conflict almost equals the value of annual development aid world wide. New aid commitments made in 2005 could be cancelled out by an increase in conflict and insecurity in the developing countries. Development and security are intimately related — one cannot be achieved without the other. DFID's approach must be guided by this.

DFID has announced its intention to develop a conflict policy to guide its efforts toward addressing conflict and achieving a more coherent approach. We welcome this initiative as an important step in ensuring that the work DFID does in conflict-prone or conflict-affected countries adds value.

DFID's work in such countries has increased in recent years. This poses new challenges for the way in which DFID delivers development assistance in difficult environments. It is important that DFID has the right tools and that is uses these tools, such as its Strategic Conflict Assessment, systematically and comprehensively. DFID must also ensure it is working coherently with other departments, and in coordination with other donors as well as the state concerned, and its civil society. Because of the high cost of conflict, and because the impacts of conflict continue after the cessation of hostilities, it is important that sufficient resources are directed towards conflict-prone and conflict-affected states. This is a necessary strategy but there are no guarantees of universal success.

The Government has developed ways of working across departments with the Conflict Prevention Pools and the Post-Conflict Reconstruction Unit. These are positive initiatives. Ways must be found to involve, in a meaningful way, the Department of Trade and Industry. This is especially the case where UK companies are trading in goods in conflict-affected countries. The current system of safeguards has been shown not to work in the Democratic Republic of Congo. The Government should also, as a matter of urgency, work towards obtaining an internationally agreed definition of conflict resources in the United Nations.

The Committee visited Sierra Leone, Uganda and the Democratic Republic of Congo. One of the lessons common to all three is that conflicts are not always contained within state boundaries. If this fact is ignored, aid given to one country may end up fuelling conflict in a neighbouring country. How a country deals with its neighbours and its role in regional tensions must form part of DFID's consideration about how much and what type of aid is suitable. Such decisions need to be reviewed regularly.

But it must be 'targetted' to achieve 'effect'

While the link between conflict and development is a relatively new field, the Government must prioritise it in order to improve development outcomes among the poorest. Preventing and ending conflicts will do more to create a climate for poverty reduction than any amount of costly aid programmes.

Acknowledgements

In November 2005 we announced our inquiry on conflict and development. The aim of the inquiry was to examine the effectiveness and external coherence of the UK's peacebuilding and post-conflict reconstruction policies with a particular focus on conflict in Africa. We received written submissions from thirty one persons and organisations including non-governmental organisations, research institutes, academics and the UK Government. We subsequently held seven evidence sessions in Parliament over a period of six months. We are grateful to all those who submitted written evidence. We would especially like to thank those who gave up their time to come and give oral evidence in Parliament.

We would also like to thank our specialist adviser, David Keen, Reader in Complex Emergencies at the Development Studies Institute, LSE. However the views expressed in this report are ours alone.

An important part of our evidence came from our visits to Sierra Leone and Uganda in February, and to the Democratic Republic of the Congo in May. We are grateful to our DFID and FCO hosts on these visits for their excellent organisation. We would also like to thank those organisations and individuals in these countries who took the time to meet with us.

1 Conflict and development

Conflict and development

1. There is an increasing recognition that the Millennium Development Goals (MDGs) will not be achieved unless more is done to prevent and resolve violent conflict.[1] Good progress has been achieved in some areas, including a decline in the number of people in poverty, but it has not been evenly spread. Sub-Saharan Africa as a whole continues to be either off-track or making slow progress toward the goals.[2]

2. Over half the countries and 20% of the population of Africa were affected by conflict in 2000. In the 1990s over six million people died and over 20 million were displaced as a direct result of conflict. And six of the top 10 countries on the 2006 Failed States Index published by *Foreign Policy*[3] are in Africa: Sudan, Democratic Republic of Congo (DRC), Côte d'Ivoire, Zimbabwe, Chad and Somalia.[4] Since the end of the Cold War the character of conflicts has changed. In seeking to prevent or resolve conflicts donor governments more and more have to engage with the internal governance and politics of these states.

3. DFID's work in conflict affected countries has increased in recent years — more money has been spent, conflict advisers have been appointed and conflict policy issues have become more prominent. The report of the Commission for Africa focused on the need for peace and security and made a number of concrete recommendations to the Government.[5] In December 2005 the UN agreed to the creation of a Peacebuilding Commission — recognition of the vital role which peacebuilding plays in ensuring that peace, once achieved, can be sustained.

4. The increasing prominence of conflict in national and international donor policies prompted us to launch an inquiry on conflict and development in November 2005. The aim of the inquiry was to examine the effectiveness and external coherence of the UK's peacebuilding and post-conflict reconstruction policies. We focussed on case studies of a number of conflicts in Africa. The evidence we collected and the conclusions we draw reflect that focus. Although there are doubtless parallels that can be drawn with conflicts elsewhere that could help inform wider peace-building and post conflict reconstruction work, we are conscious that conflicts in different places have different characteristics and often require different responses. We therefore recommend caution in trying to apply "off the shelf theories" when assessing the appropriate responses to conflicts in different parts of the world.

5. We decided to visit three countries at different stages of conflict, and where DFID has significant programmes: Sierra Leone — to explore DFID's efforts at post-conflict reconstruction; Uganda — which has an ongoing conflict in the north, but which in all

---

1   Ev 151 (SaferWorld)

2   Jeffrey Sachs, *Investing in Development: A Practical Plan To Achieve The Development Goals,* 17 January 2005, pp 28-29.

3   A US magazine published by the Carnegie Endowment for International Peace, Washington DC

4   Lord Triesman, *Democracy and Security in Africa*, Speech at Chatham House, June 21, 2006.

5   Commission for Africa, *Our Common Interest: Report of the Commission for Africa*, March 2005, Chapter 5

other respects is a country whose poverty reduction programme is functioning well; and the Democratic Republic of Congo (DRC) — which, despite a formal peace agreement, experiences continued low-level fighting in parts of the country and high rates of conflict-related mortality. These visits gave us the opportunity to see first-hand the UK Government's approach to peacebuilding and post-conflict reconstruction in practice.

Human Security

6. Violent conflict can result from a wide range of social, political and economic conditions.[6] Of particular significance for donors is the link between a rapid decline in national income and the onset of conflict. Research suggests on average a negative economic growth shock of 5% increases civil war risks by about 50%.[7] Conflict also has huge negative implications for economic growth. Paul Collier, Professor of Economics at Oxford University, estimates that for a low income country the average cost of a civil war is about US$54 billion, and that in addition there are global costs, more difficult to quantify, associated with each civil war[8]. This compares with the total global aid budget of US$78.6 billion in 2004.[9] The implications of these findings are that increasing economic growth rates, and income, can significantly reduce the risk of conflict, which in turn potentially saves billions of dollars for these countries. These economic correlations are significant — poor states tend to be weak states and weak states are more vulnerable to conflict.[10] The quests for security and development are integrally related.

7. The concept of human security was first developed as an international policy framework in the 1994 *Human Development Report* of the UN Development Programme. The report sought to shift the framework for thinking about security away from one with a primary focus on the external security of the state towards one which focused on the security of the individual within a given state. The 1994 *Human Development Report* defined human security as "safety from such chronic threats as hunger, disease and repression, and protection from sudden and hurtful disruptions in the patterns of daily lives."[11] This represented a significant shift in approach to security, because it inserted what had traditionally been the concerns of the development community into the agendas of military and strategic planners, as well as diplomats, and vice versa.[12] Whereas the pursuit of development is often equated with the goal of poverty reduction, and security with the protection of state sovereignty, the idea of human security involves a recognition that "development goes into reverse if people do not feel secure and lasting security cannot be achieved if people do not see development taking place."[13] This has implications for the

---

6   Ev 151 (Saferworld)

7   Memorandum submitted by Professor Robert Picciotto, printed in International Development Committee, Conflict and Development, HC 464- i, 15 March 2005. See also Collier, P and Hoffler, A , On Economic causes of civil war, *Oxford Economic Papers* 50:563-73, 1998.

8   Paul Collier, *ibid.*

9   www.globalissues.org using figures from the OECD.

10   For a more detailed discussion about the economic and political causes of civil wars see Chapter 3 of this report, Building the Peace.

11   UNDP *Human Development Report 1994, New Dimensions of Human Development,*

12   Robert Picciotto, et al *Global Development and Human Security: towards a policy agenda*, Ministry of Foreign Affairs, Sweden 2005, p iv

13   Robert Picciotto, et al *Global Development and Human Security*, p 1

possibility of achieving the Millennium Development Goals (MDGs). The efforts that the international community has put into increasing international aid in 2005 could be cancelled out by an increase in conflict and insecurity in the developing world.

8. By 2005 human security had become the theme of two important UN reports — the report of the Secretary General's High Level Panel on Threats, Challenges and Change, and the Secretary General's own report, *In Larger Freedom*. The latter report led to agreement at the 2005 World Summit on the creation of a Peacebuilding Commission, a new Human Rights Council, and on the existence of the principle of the Responsibility to Protect. All three are potentially important for human security. For example, the report argues that there is a shared responsibility for the provision of global security so that when states commit crimes against their own citizens, or fail to protect them, the international community has a responsibility to protect those citizens. The Responsibility to Protect thus challenges the longstanding principle of non-intervention and gives the international community greater responsibilities to act to protect civilians where states fail to do so.

The Securitization of Development

9. Although the human security agenda aims to reduce and ultimately eliminate those factors that prevent the attainment of secure living conditions, the idea of human security has more recently been defined as "a set of discursive practices by which the international community of effective states understands and intervenes within ineffective ones." [14] In this understanding failed, fragile or weak states are seen to present a threat to international stability and this threat has to be contained in recognition of an increasingly interconnected world. Indeed, to some, maintaining "international stability" is regarded as synonymous with the security needs of individual states. It is summed up in the following quote from the American journal, *Foreign Affairs*: "there is a crisis of governance in a large number of weak, impoverished states, and this crisis poses a serious threat to US national security."[15]   The new thinking is frequently referred to as 'the securitization of development' and has become prevalent since the 'war on terror' after the 9/11 attack on the US.

10. The relationship between poverty, inequality and the causes of terrorism in the Middle East and elsewhere is complex and goes well beyond the focus of this report. In relation to Africa, however, we question the wisdom of simplistically securitizing development issues. Research by the Centre for Global Development, for example, questions the link between poor states and the spread of international terrorism:

> "it has become conventional wisdom that poorly performing states generate multiple cross-border 'spillovers', including terrorism, weapons proliferation, organized crime, regional instability, global pandemics, and energy insecurity. What is striking is how little empirical evidence underpins such sweeping assertions. A

---

14   Mark Duffield, *Human Security: development, containment and re-territorialization*, Chatham House ISP/NSC Briefing Paper 05/02, October 2005.

15   S. Eizenstat et al Rebuilding Weak States, *Foreign Affairs*, vol 84 no 1 January/February 2005.

closer look suggests that the connection between state weakness and global threats is less clear and more variable than typically assumed."[16]

11. The idea of human security — linking the spheres of security and development — should form one of the building blocks for policies towards weak and failing states. However, it is important that "northern" security assumptions should not be allowed to distort or undermine efforts to promote security and poverty reduction in Africa in line with DFID's Public Service Agreement and the MDGs.

The Committee's visits

Sierra Leone

12. In February 2006 the Committee visited Sierra Leone and Uganda. In Sierra Leone we found a relatively peaceful post-conflict country which had received significant assistance — initially military and subsequently developmental — from the UK. The UK remains the largest single donor, and given a lack of donor coordination, often the donor of first and last resort.

13. Our visit to Sierra Leone involved meetings with the UN Agencies, visits to alluvial diamond mining areas and to a multinational company undertaking kimberlite mining in Koidu. We held discussions about the future security of Sierra Leone and looked in particular at the way the army and the police were working together under the guidance of the International Military Advisory and Training Team (IMATT). We met the Anti-corruption Commissioner and visited the Special Court.

14. We were impressed by the progress that Sierra Leone has made in the three years since the end of its last conflict. This progress has been aided significantly by the efforts of donors, amongst whom DFID has played a leading role. Progress remains fragile however. Many of the factors identified to us as causes of the conflict remain present in Sierra Leone, including: high levels of unemployment (particularly among young men); the concentration of power (social and political) in the hands of a small, corrupt, elite; and, the country's wealth of alluvial diamonds.

15. DFID's programme in Sierra Leone has grown since the end of the war in 2002, and the UK Government now has a ten year partnership agreement with the Government of Sierra Leone, fulfilling its commitment to long-term predictability of aid flows. DFID's programme is undergoing a shift in emphasis; from its immediate post-conflict focus on security sector reform and infrastructure rebuilding towards a greater investment in building accountability and good governance, and encouraging private sector development. Our meetings with local community leaders in Koidu demonstrated that this shift, from highly visible assistance to largely invisible support, is likely to have a significant impact on the ways in which DFID's contribution is perceived. **DFID may need to give more thought to the wider 'public relations' impact of the shift away from highly visible support to less visible assistance in post-conflict countries, especially in those where it is**

---

16   Stewart Patrick, *Weak states and global threats: assessing evidence of spillover*. Working Paper no 73 Centre for Global Development, January 2006.

the largest bilateral donor. If peace is to be viable, it is important that people perceive both immediate and sustained benefits from it.

Uganda

16. In Uganda there has been a 20 year conflict in the north of the country involving in the main, the Lord's Resistance Army (LRA). The conflict has resulted in the displacement of approximately 1.7 million people, who now live in internally displaced persons (IDP) camps, which are maintained largely by UN agencies. We visited two camps in Gulu district. The accommodation is basic — mud huts with thatched roofs, built close together, which frequently catch fire. There are schools but insufficient teachers and health centres but few doctors. The police presence is minimal and wholly inadequate. The water supply is erratic, and the public health statistics are among the worst in the world. A 2005 survey by the World Health Organisation (WHO) found that the crude and under-five mortality rates among children were well above expected emergency rates. Malaria, AIDS and violence are the three main causes of death in under-fives, but there are also high levels of water-borne and transmittable diseases, as well as malnutrition.[17] In recent months there have been outbreaks of cholera in a number of the camps.

17. According to the Civil Society Organisations for Peace in Northern Uganda, the conflict causes up to 130 deaths per day.[18] WHO estimates that 12,000 children have been abducted by the LRA since June 2002.[19] The boys are trained to become soldiers and the girls are taken as wives and/or slaves. Girls are also made to fight and commit atrocities. During our visit we met some returned abducted children and heard their harrowing tales. These children were being reintegrated into their families and communities despite the likelihood of their having participated in atrocities against their own people.

18. We were told that the security situation has improved over the last year. In particular, the LRA has lost its safe haven in southern Sudan since the Comprehensive Peace Agreement brought the civil war there to a formal end. Unfortunately, this has led the LRA to seek refuge in northern DRC, itself a conflict affected area. The Government of Uganda and the UN are overseeing the voluntary decampment of some IDPs to smaller camps which are nearer to the IDPs' original villages. The process is not without its problems and camps in Teso had to be disbanded following attacks by the LRA. In the past six months improved security has enabled IDPs to reach land further away from the camps and around the satellite camps, and to cultivate crops and livestock.

19. The level of fear brought about by the conflict has also created the phenomenon of 'night commuters' — children who leave their homes at nightfall to sleep, together with other children, sometimes up to a hundred in a large room, in order that they may be protected from abduction by the LRA. Improved security has dramatically reduced the numbers of night commuters although some children still do so for social reasons.

---

17   World Health Organization, *Health and Mortality Survey among Internally Displaced Persons*, Geneva: WHO, 2005.

18   HC Deb, 20 June, col 388 Westminster Hall.

19   World Health Organisation, 2005 *op cit.*

20. The cost of running the IDP camps in northern Uganda is largely borne by UN agencies. We were told that the cost of running the camps was US$200 million a year. Although the camps clearly meet a need, their continued existence brings with it the risk of institutionalising those who live in them. Northern Ugandans are at risk of losing their agricultural skills and other livelihood strategies as they have become more dependent on the international community to provide for them.   In addition, with the international community continuing to provide resources for the camps, the pressure is taken off the Government of Uganda to provide for its own citizens. In effect the international community is paying US$200 million per year to provide services which the Government of Uganda should either be providing or for which there would be no demand if the IDPs could go about their normal daily lives.

21. In Uganda DFID is supporting a government which is making reasonable progress in poverty reduction, education and health in the south of the country, but which is not able to exercise effectively key governance functions in the north of the country. In addition we were concerned about the attitude of some Ugandan Government officials towards the DRC. Uganda also has a history of involvement in the conflict in the DRC.   A senior Foreign Ministry official expressed to us, in strong words, the view that the DRC was a failed state and that it had effectively forfeited its sovereignty.   Another member of the Government of Uganda said that hot pursuit of the LRA into the DRC was permissible.

22. We consider that insufficient international pressure has been put on the Government of Uganda to work towards either a negotiated or a military solution to the conflict. In January 2006 the UK Government withheld £15 million of its 2005–6 Poverty Reduction Budget Support (PRBS) to the Government of Uganda, because of concerns about the way in which the first multiparty elections were being handled, and diverted £10 million of this to assist with the humanitarian crisis in the north. Following our visit, in July 2006, the UK Government announced that budget support for 2006–7 to the Government of Uganda would be kept at £35 million, the 2005–6 level.[20]

23. **We accept that the continuing conflict in northern Uganda is not the fault of the Government of Uganda. Nevertheless the Government of Uganda has responsibilities to its population in the north which hitherto it has failed to fulfil. Instead of meeting its responsibilities, the Government of Uganda has been relying on donors to provide core functions such as health and education. This is costing donors US$200 million per year — money which could make a huge development impact if the conflict was resolved and the resources were spent on post-war reconstruction and on resettling displaced people in their villages.**

24. Since the Committee's visit in February there have been peace negotiations brokered by the Government of South Sudan taking place in Juba. Peace talks have failed before but for a number of reasons these appear more promising than at any time since the LRA started its campaign 20 years ago. There is a general belief that peace will allow security to be re-established more comprehensively than a military solution. If security is re-established in northern Uganda we understand that the population would prefer to return to the land

---

20   Hilary Benn MP, DFID Written Ministerial Statement, *Uganda: Poverty Reduction Budget Support,* 3 July 2006

rather than to decongestion camps as previously proposed by the Government of Uganda. These would only find favour if peace was not fully established.

25. Peace in northern Uganda would require the current aid budget to be diverted to development as people re-establish their livelihoods on the land. Aid would be needed for clean water, tools, seeds and re-establishing livestock on a well-watered and fertile part of Uganda that has the capacity to feed itself and export cash crops to the benefit of the whole of Uganda, which faces a population explosion.

26. Rivalry between the north which supports the opposition and the south would require the donor community to ensure that development aid is concentrated on building livelihoods in the north and not diverted for political favours in the south.

Democratic Republic of Congo

27. During our visit to the Democratic Republic of Congo (DRC), only two months before the delayed elections, we experienced a country, larger than Western Europe, with an ineffective Transitional Government. We spent two days in Kinshasa before flying east to Bukavu in South Kivu district. It was clear that the Transitional Government was unable to control large parts of the country, particularly the east, where militia groups still operate. DRC is host to the largest ever UN peacekeeping mission, MONUC, with a force of 17,000. Unfortunately, and despite some good efforts, MONUC has been plagued by accusations of improper conduct.

28. The DFID programme in the DRC has grown from £7 million in 2001–02 to £55 million with a projected increase to £70 million in 2007–08. DFID is now the largest bilateral donor in the DRC. Nearly half of the DFID programme is directed at humanitarian assistance, reflecting severe and ongoing needs in this sector. Most of the remainder of DFID funding currently goes on attempts to establish security, the rule of law, and a functioning state. Support for preparations for the July 2006 elections falls into the latter category. After the elections DFID is planning to produce a full Country Assistance Plan which will include more emphasis on post-conflict reconstruction and the management of natural resources.

29. The Government has announced its intention to develop a conflict policy and this report sets out many of the key issues which we think should be considered in the writing of this policy. Chapter Two looks at DFID's current policies and its approach towards conflict-prone and conflict-affected (CPCA) states. In Chapter Three we ask the question how can the UK Government make its development policies more conflict-sensitive and contribute towards sustainable peace in CPCA states? We are aware that no matter how conflict-sensitive the UK Government's policies, they will not have an impact unless they form part of a global effort. Coherence within the international community, including multilateral donors, is a prerequisite for successful peacebuilding and post-conflict reconstruction. This is the subject of Chapter Four. Chapter Five focuses on the role of the newly-formed UN Peacebuilding Commission.

2 The UK Government's approach to conflict

30. DFID has announced its intention to develop a conflict policy. The consultation document issued in advance of the policy notes that although DFID is at the forefront of addressing conflict, there is no common understanding of conflict issues across DFID so that in effect the whole of DFID's efforts on conflict is often less than the sum of its parts.[21]

31. The consultation document identifies three main areas for improvement in DFID's practice: 1) greater focus on conflict prevention, 2) new ways of providing conflict-sensitive aid in difficult circumstances and 3) increasing the quality and effectiveness of DFID's on-going conflict work. The document acknowledges that as more DFID funding goes to CPCA states it will have to find ways of ensuring that progress can be made on its primary goal of poverty alleviation while also ensuring that aid is conflict-sensitive. The recent OECD Development Assistance Committee (DAC) peer review notes DFID's leadership role in policy on fragile states. However, the review also states that the lack of a conflict policy prevents DFID's good work on fragile states being integrated into its work on conflict prevention.[22] We commend the decision to develop a conflict policy to guide DFID's efforts addressing conflict and contribute towards a more coherent approach to conflict.

DFID's approach to conflict

32. Conflict policy issues are mainly handled by DFID's Conflict, Humanitarian Affairs and Security Department (CHASE)[23] located in the United Nations, Conflict and Humanitarian Division. There are also three Geographic Divisions (Africa, Asia and Europe, Middle East and Americas) which play a role in shaping DFID's conflict policies. Within the Africa Division there is also an Africa Conflict and Humanitarian Unit (ACHU). In April 2003 DFID's policy division established a Poverty Reduction in Difficult Environments team to lead DFID policy on fragile states. This team is now called the Fragile States team.

33. DFID's approach to conflict is informed by the three DFID White Papers as well as two 2005 publications, *Why we need to work more effectively in fragile states,*[24] and *Fighting poverty to build a safer world.*[25] Both publications reaffirm DFID's commitment to working in CPCA states as an integral part of its commitment to poverty elimination. They also maintain the existence of a link between terrorism and international crime, and conflict in developing countries, reflecting the securitization of development concerns discussed in

---

21   DFID, Policy Concept Note: addressing Conflict to Reduce Poverty, 2006.

22   OECD, *DAC Peer Review: United Kingdom*, OECD, Development Assistance Committee, 2006.

23   Formerly CHAD – conflict and humanitarian affairs. The inclusion of security into the rubric of activities is a response to increased concerns about the link between CPCA states and international security.

24   DFID, *Why we need to work more effectively in fragile states*, January 2005.

25   DFID, *Fighting Poverty to build a safer world*, March 2005.

Chapter One. Both argue that development and security goals should be pursued in a mutually reinforcing way.

Engaging with fragile states

34. *Why we need to work more effectively in fragile states* suggests that 46 states, containing 870 million people or 14% of the world's population, are fragile — countries where the government cannot or will not deliver core functions to the majority of its population. It is these states, DFID notes, which are most off-track in relation to achieving the MDGs. Moreover, fragile states tend to destabilise, or be destabilised by, their neighbours. For these reasons DFID intends to place increased focus on such states.

35. There is no definitive list of states that are termed fragile although most donors, including DFID, use the World Bank's Country Policy and Institutional Assessment (CPIA) index. This divides states into five categories of performance and the lowest two are used as proxies for state fragility. One of our witnesses, Robert Picciotto, cautioned that the World Bank's is not a good index because it measures state performance and this has contributed inevitably to the creation of 'aid orphans'— countries which do not receive a lot of development assistance, and 'aid darlings' — countries which are rewarded for performing well.[26] Not all fragile states are engaged in conflict, but all states which are engaged in or are emerging from conflict are fragile. This inquiry is focused on states which have recently emerged from, or are in the process of, emerging from conflict — what we have termed conflict-prone and conflict-affected (CPCA) states.

36. Engaging in fragile states is costly, difficult and risky.[27] The fear of failure and the need to satisfy the domestic electorate that aid is performing well leads donors towards countries that have sound policies and institutions and away from fragile states where policies and institutions are weak. Robert Picciotto also told us that "although it will be politically difficult to argue for greater risk taking, to get the best results you have to look at aid as venture capital. If you can prevent one war, it means $60 billion in the bank."[28] A recent OECD report notes that fragile states continue to receive less aid than other comparable low income countries.[29] At present somewhere in the region of 10-15% of ODA is spent in what are termed fragile states.[30] This is nowhere near enough to reduce the incidence of conflict in developing countries.

37. If the MDGs are to be achieved in all developing countries, increasingly donors will have to operate in CPCA states. **The evidence we received in hearings and on our visits leads us to believe that CPCA states are precisely where a large part of development assistance should be focused, and we support DFID in this regard. However, this new approach entails significant risks for DFID — some programmes may not achieve the desired results, others will take much longer than anticipated. DFID cannot work alone in this; it must ensure it has the support of other government departments. The human**

---

26   Q 161 (Prof Picciotto, Kings College, London)

27   DFID, *Why we need to work more effectively in fragile states*, January 2005.

28   Q 159 (Prof Picciotto, Kings College, London)

29   OECD, *Monitoring Resource Flows to Fragile States* 2005 Report. DCD(2006)1, 2 June 2006.

30   Q 159, Q160 (Prof Picciotto, Kings College, London)

security approach discussed in Chapter One explicitly demands greater coherence across the whole of Government.

Building-up effective and accountable states

38. DFID's 2006 White Paper, *Making governance work for the poor*[31] says that effective states are necessary to provide security for the population. For these reasons DFID intends to focus on building up effective and accountable institutions as part of its approach to improving security. Government institutions in the DRC have historically been predatory and exploitative of the population. Countering state fragility is thus a key objective of the DFID programme in the DRC. Consequently DFID has supported the holding of elections as an essential first step towards improving state-society relations and legitimising the government. In the longer term DFID also intends to support government capacity to deliver in a particular social service.[32]

39. DFID notes that in the post-conflict period countries are most able to absorb aid about four years after the end of the conflict, when growth rates have increased, but that this is precisely the period when donors begin to consider cutting back on their aid, as we witnessed first hand in the DRC. The UK Government has consequently made ten-year commitments to both Sierra Leone and Rwanda. Such assurances signal that the UK has made a long-term commitment to continue supporting the post-conflict reconstruction process.

40. DFID has reinforced its commitment by using budget support as a mechanism for delivering funds to these states. The evidence we have received persuades us that it is right to provide governments in post-conflict states with a long-term development assistance commitment, especially when they are making good progress in key poverty reduction indicators, but it is important that donors constantly re-evaluate the methods and objectives of this assistance. The provision of poverty reduction budget support to Sierra Leone in the immediate aftermath of the conflict was appropriate given the country's need for extensive investment in reconstruction, and the Government's limited tax-raising powers. A few years on, however, it appears that the continuing provision of PRBS may be entrenching the powers of a political elite and limiting the incentive for them to implement urgently needed governance reforms.

41. We agree with recent changes in HMG's approach to conditionality, away from policy conditionality, but the situation in Sierra Leone demonstrates that DFID can only exert limited leverage on the Government to make the changes needed to reduce corruption, facilitate effective governance and promote development in Sierra Leone. This indicates the importance for DFID teams of prioritising their strategic planning when operating in a post-conflict country — the need constantly to re-evaluate the appropriateness of policies and adjust their operations accordingly. DFID needs to give more thought to the timing and sequencing of the type of aid it employs in countries recently emerged from conflict if it wishes to create more effective states.

---

31 DFID, *Making governance work for the poor*, July 2006, p 45. Available online at http://www.DFID.gov.uk/wp2006/whitepaper-printer-friendly.pdf

32 DFID, DFID and conflict in the DRC: Analysis and response, April 2006.

42. We draw similar conclusions on UK Government policy in Rwanda, although the circumstances here are different. The UK Government is the largest bilateral donor in Rwanda providing £46 million in 2005/6, with two-thirds of this being given as budget support. There is a general consensus that the Rwandan Government is making good progress on poverty reduction, but there are concerns about its behaviour toward the DRC. A UN Panel report in 2002 indicated that budget support to Rwanda was causing problems for the DRC. The report on the illegal exploitation of resources from the DRC called for a reduction of development assistance to countries implicated in DRC exploitation.[33]

43. The Government of Rwanda has committed itself to ensuring that the operations of armed Rwandan militias in the DRC, including the FDLR[34], are curtailed. On our visit to DRC in May 2006 it was clear that some pro-Rwandan militia groups were also still causing problems in the east of the country. In 2004 for example, the town of Bukavu had been briefly taken over by renegade officers formerly in the RCD-Goma[35] army despite the presence of MONUC forces.

44. The UK Government response when questioned about the provision of budget support to the Government of Rwanda was that it engaged in a constant process of judgement and decision making and that on balance the UK Government judged Rwanda's behaviour to be satisfactory.[36]

45. **We recognise that there are difficult policy dilemmas for donors working in countries emerging from conflict, and that 'good enough' government is often a worthwhile achievement.[37] DFID should ensure that it is not excusing wrongful acts as aberrations in an otherwise successful development partnership.**

Evaluating Conflict

The conflict cycle

46. The need to build up better functioning states intersects with the need for donor policies to be effective and coordinated. Donor countries' engagement with conflict-affected countries is often governed by an approach which tends to draw boundaries between conflict management, reconstruction and development. But in many instances humanitarian aid, post-conflict rehabilitation and development finance need to be run in parallel to deliver results. In practice, conflicts do not move predictably from one phase to another, and the demands of donors at any one stage are often multidimensional.

47. In evidence submitted to the Committee on an earlier inquiry, Robert Picciotto warned that simplistic depictions of the conflict cycle had contributed to a lack of synergy in CPCA states:

---

33   UN, *UN Panel Report on the illegal exploitation of resources and other forms of wealth from the DRC*, S/2002/1146.

34   Forces Démocratique pour la Libération du Rwanda

35   Rally for Congolese Democracy (RCD). This was the original rebel movement which attacked the Kabila regime. It was assembled by Rwanda and Uganda and made up of anti–Kabila elements. The RCD-Goma maintains close ties with Rwanda although it is now part of the transitional Government.

36   Q 95 (Mr Evans, DFID)

37   DFID, *Why we need to work more effectively in fragile states.*

"The 'conflict cycle' construct does not fit insurgencies that continue well after the conventional battlefield war has been won (Afghanistan, Iraq); to prolonged civil wars fed by illicit use of natural resources (DRC) to the violence of collapsed states (Haiti), or to long drawn out civil wars that pit one ethnic or religious group against another (Sudan)."[38]

48. Christian Aid also commented on the tendency of donors to have separate and sometimes uncoordinated approaches to different stages of a conflict.[39] The danger inherent in the cyclical approach to conflict is that certain programmes may be delayed until the appropriate stage is arrived at or withdrawn prematurely when a given stage is deemed to have ended. We saw an example of this during our visit to the DRC where we visited the Panzi Hospital in Bukavu. Although some donors judge the humanitarian crisis to be over, we saw first-hand evidence of the way in which militia groups operating in eastern DRC continue to perpetrate sexual violence on women. The women in the hospital were awaiting or recovering from operations. About ten women per day were still being admitted to the hospital including many who had walked for days to get there. The hospital was filling an evident and continuing need in the area but we were told it is at risk of closing because funding from the European Commission Humanitarian Office (ECHO) and the US is due to be stopped shortly as both agencies view the humanitarian crisis as being over. This shows the dangers of donors adopting a cyclical approach to conflict. We have since been told that ECHO is undertaking an assessment of the continued demand for the hospital.[40]

49. There is a danger of donors assuming that conflict is over with the signing of formal peace accords and consequently not paying sufficient attention to the implementation of the peace agreement. For example in Sudan, details of who gets the oil revenues, and the slow pace of demobilisation of government soldiers in the south have not been high on the international community's agenda. Instead, it could be argued that the ongoing crisis in Darfur has taken attention away from the implementation of these peace accords in the same way that — at an earlier stage — the prospect of a peace settlement to the conflict in the south of Sudan took attention away from Darfur, weakening international pressure on Khartoum because international actors didn't want to jeopardize the southern Sudan peace process.[41]

50. Questions about the distribution of humanitarian assistance should be based on need, rather than the particular theoretical stage of a conflict. Such funding should be wound down as needs decrease. ECHO should ensure that key facilities such as the Panzi Hospital are not closed prematurely. Conflict-related services, such as the unit for women victims of sexual violence, will be needed for years to come. Similarly the signing of peace accords should not take international attention and funding away from the process of their implementation. While the cyclical approach is a useful tool, a more integrated approach to the whole of conflict would produce better outcomes.

---

38   Robert Picciotto, Memorandum printed in International Development Committee, *Conflict and Development,* HC 464-i

39   Ev 165 (Christian Aid)

40   Ev 124 (DFID)

41   International Development Committee, Third Report of Session 2005-6, *Darfur: the Killing Continues* HC 657.

Conflict assessments

51. Donors need the correct tools to deliver increasing amounts of development assistance effectively and in a timely manner. One way of helping to ensure that development assistance is effective in CPCA states is to carry out an assessment prior to the start of engagement. Such assessments usually include an analysis of the causal factors of the conflict, the parties to the conflict, the effects of the conflict on different groups, and what policies would be most effective at preventing a return to conflict.

52. DFID has developed its own conflict assessment tool, the Strategic Conflict Assessment (SCA). DFID report that:

> "our use of SCAs has not only begun to improve our own bilateral approach to conflict, it has been influential in steering other international actors, such as the World Bank, towards adopting more conflict-sensitive policies and practice." [42]

53. The tool is not used systematically however — for example, there has been one tool for assessing northern Uganda, but not one for the whole of Uganda.[43] Nor is it always clear that the results are used in the formulation of development policy.[44] Saferworld told us that:

> "there is this conflict assessment framework but it has not been used comprehensively or used to its full strength, and when it has been done in certain countries it has not necessarily translated into the development programme being adjusted based on what has been found from the assessment."[45]

54. Evidence submitted by ActionAid supports the use of the SCA by DFID but considers that "there is too much dependency on the analysis of outside consultants and not enough on ensuring that there are channels through which poor people can enable their understanding of their own situation to be known."[46] ActionAid have pioneered Participatory Vulnerability Analysis (PVA) whereby poor communities, with the help of local facilitators and outside experts, collectively articulate those factors contributing to their own vulnerable situations. The PVA will also identify what can be done about these factors, and in particular what the community itself can do. John Abuya, Director of ActionAid's Great Lakes programme, told us in his evidence about the way in which this PVA was used in Rwanda and the DRC and how it had encouraged people to be open and frank about the issues which were of concern to them. The process is at an early stage — follow up and implementation has not yet been completed.[47] **We believe that DFID should pay greater attention to local knowledge and local points of view in their SCA tool. While we recognise that conflict theories can help inform analysis, we would expect DFID to acknowledge the distinctive character of each conflict and to listen to local people.**

---

42 Ev 108 (DFID)

43 Q 9 (Claire Hickson, Saferworld)

44 Ev 118-119 (DFID)

45 Q 2 (Claire Hickson, Saferworld)

46 Ev 126 (ActionAid)

47 Q 251 (John Abuya, ActionAid)

55. Robert Picciotto told us that there was no independent evaluation of the effectiveness of the SCA. He said "it (DFID) has an evaluation system; but it is not independent. You need an independent evaluation system that checks whether or not the conflict assessments are making a difference or are they simply writing a report which is put on the shelf."[48]

56. Conflict assessments should be a precondition for engaging in CPCA states and mandatory for all donors. There is no reason why donors should not share the results of such assessments, rather than duplicating efforts. Conflict assessment is a necessary but not a sufficient guarantor of effective development assistance — measures need to be put in place to ensure that the analysis informs policy. The whole of HMG should make use of the analysis resulting from the conflict assessment — it should not be restricted to DFID. In addition, there should be independent evaluations of how well conflict assessments are done.

Conflict-sensitive aid

57. The delivery of basic services is difficult in situations of conflict often requiring a conflict-specific approach. Aid agencies and donors may take on this role in the short to medium term until the government is capable of so doing. Increasingly donors such as DFID also seek to provide a 'peace dividend' in the aftermath of conflict in order to meet some of the material expectations of the population, especially those who have laid down their arms. For example, in the DRC the exclusion and deprivation of the majority of the population is met by DFID support for improved access to healthcare and water for war-affected populations. In addition, DFID has invested in a road rehabilitation project. This had to be put on hold subsequently because of local political corruption.[49] There is a larger donor-driven reconstruction programme in eastern DRC which is not yet fully up and running. In its efforts to counter war economies, which have been a powerful incentive for conflict in the DRC, DFID has supported the Extractive Industries Transparency Initiative (EITI). However long delays on the part of the transitional Government mean that the EITI is not yet off the ground in the DRC.[50] The importance of linking aid and trade and investment policy in CPCA states is discussed in more detail in Chapter Three.

58. Aid can exacerbate conflict if it fails to take into account human and security considerations — the potential marginalisation of certain communities, the distribution of income, as well as the wider regional context of the conflict.[51] In its efforts to build up effective states, conflict-sensitive aid should take into account the immediate and long term impact of development assistance on communities affected by conflict including the economic, political and societal implications. Too often donors fail to recognise the link between aid and conflict and impose donor-driven agendas with little appreciation of the local context.[52] In the DRC we noted the irony of local NGOs and local representatives of international NGOs looking for some conditionality from the donor community, having long argued for aid to be completely untied. It is important that the donor community as a

---

48 Q 165 (Prof Picciotto, Kings College, London)

49   DFID, *DFID and conflict in the DRC: analysis and response*, April 2006.

50   Global Witness, *Digging for corruption*, July 2006 p. 12

51   Q 10 (Oli Brown, IISD)

52   Ev 143, (IISD)

whole is working together to ensure that the whole package of assistance is coordinated and coherent. In addition it needs to work in cooperation with recipient governments and/or the private sector.[53]

59. However, because aid represents a decreasing part of donor involvement in developing countries, the impact on non-aid policies in CPCA states needs also to be examined. Robert Picciotto has suggested that aid can be used as leverage for other policies. In the same way that aid-for-trade has become part of the WTO agenda,[54] aid for migration or aid for adaptation to global warming could also be encouraged.[55] It is unusual, we were told, to find country strategies to which the whole of the donor government subscribed.[56]

Policy coherence across the Government

60. In written evidence, DFID states that the Government aims to combine different perspectives from foreign policy, defence and international development to tackle the causes and consequences of conflict. To this end there is a Public Service Agreement objective shared by these Departments which sets out the aim:

> "by 2008, to deliver improved effectiveness of UK and international support in conflict prevention by addressing the long term structural causes of conflict, managing regional and national tension and violence, and supporting post-conflict reconstruction, where the UK can make a significant contribution, in particular Africa, Asia, Balkans and the Middle East."[57]

61. In 2001 the Government set up the Conflict Prevention Pools (CPPs) jointly with the MoD and the FCO in order to improve the UK's effectiveness in conflict prevention. There are two Pools — a Global Pool (GCPP) which is chaired by the Foreign Secretary, and the Africa Pool (ACPP) chaired by the Secretary of State for International Development. Both are supported by the Treasury and the Cabinet Office. The Pools are a small part of the Government's overall funding for reducing conflict. The GCPP for example has an annual budget of about £80 million and the ACPP £60 million. Neither of the Pools involves the Department of Trade and Industry or any other Departments. In the following Chapter we provide evidence of why we think the DTI, for example, should be more closely involved in the Government's objectives with regard to CPCA states.[58] In particular, we would like the DTI to take a more proactive role on conflict and development issues especially in the fields of conflict resources and tackling bribery and corruption.

---

53   Ev 125 (ActionAid)

54   International Development Committee, Third Report of Session 2005-6, *The WTO Hong Kong Ministerial and the Doha Development Agenda*, HC 730.

55   Q 162 (Prof Picciotto, King's College, London)

56   Q 162 (Prof Picciotto, King's College, London)

57   Ev 106 (DFID)

58   DFID also has a stake in the cross-departmental Post-Conflict Reconstruction Unit (PCRU) which was established in 2004 largely in response to failures in Iraq, in particular the failure of the Coalition forces to plan for what would happen immediately after the war was over. The PCRU is usually to be used where significant UK forces are engaged – to date only in Afghanistan. It has not therefore formed part of this inquiry.

62. The Government's objectives for the Africa Conflict Prevention Pool are:

- to support the building of African conflict management capacity,

- to assist with conflict prevention, management and post-conflict reconstruction in a number of priority sub-regions and country conflicts, and

- to support pan-African initiatives for security sector reform, small arms control and to address the economic and financial causes of conflict.[59]

While the Government holds up the Pools as models of inter-departmental cooperation, the projects funded by the Pools are relatively small, usually less than £5 million, and there is no mechanism for up-scaling the projects.

63. The Pools were independently evaluated in 2004.[60] The evaluation found that the Pools had encouraged inter-departmental cooperation and a sharing of policy analysis both in Whitehall and in the field, especially in Africa where decision making is largely delegated to DFID country offices. The evaluation also pointed out that the Pools were often seen by the individual Departments as a means of keeping their own old projects going when departmental funding was no longer available, and that the Global Pool, appeared to have a different operational culture from the Africa Pool. This indicates that although three different arms of the Government are cooperating in terms of accessing funds, and indeed in agreeing such funding, they may in fact retain distinct and sometimes contradictory goals. For example in many post-conflict environments the MoD will fund Quick Impact Projects (QIPs). These are short-term projects designed to build good will among the local population for the UK forces — winning hearts and minds. DFID will only fund QIPs if they have a poverty reduction objective. DFID wrote to us saying that 'winning hearts and minds' is a military concept which DFID cannot support.[61] Nevertheless DFID has funded a number of MoD QIPs, in Iraq for example, designed essentially for force protection, but which can simultaneously meet humanitarian, post-conflict stabilisation or recovery needs. This does raise questions about whose objectives are being met.

64. The Development Assistance Committee (DAC) of the Organisation for Economic Cooperation and Development (OECD) also commented on the need for greater cooperation and sharing of goals between all Government departments in CPCA states.[62] A single Cabinet sub-committee on conflict prevention and reconstruction met for the first time in March 2006 as part of the effort to support more coherent cross-departmental initiatives on conflict. **We welcome the continuation of the Conflict Prevention Pools, which are a small but important part of the Government's approach to conflict. They provide an important channel for inter-departmental cooperation in CPCA states, itself a prerequisite for greater effectiveness of HMG actions in difficult environments. However, because the Pools fund relatively small departmental projects they do not by themselves demonstrate a joined-up approach. Policy coherence is desirable but it is important to be clear about the policy around which coherence is sought.**

---

59   DFID, *The ACCP: an information document*, September 2004.

60   DFID, *Evaluation of Conflict Prevention Pools*, March 2004.

61   Ev 121 (DFID)

62   This sentiment is also shared by the DAC peer review, p 89.

65. **We agree that DFID should not commit its resources to "winning hearts and minds", but we understand why it is often necessary for peacekeeping troops to implement quick impact projects to win support from local people. As an exercise in joined-up government, military commanders should consult DFID, and other development agencies, about their proposals for quick impact projects, to try to ensure that they deliver development as well as security benefits.**

The importance of Security Sector Reform (SSR)

66. Security Sector Reform (SSR), aimed at ensuring effective security institutions operating under democratic control, plays a crucially important role in post-conflict settings without which very little developmental progress is possible. SSR is concerned with reforms of the bodies that provide security to the people — the armed forces, the police — as well as the state institutions responsible for managing these bodies. The largest part of programme expenditure on the ACPP is allocated for post-conflict security sector reform — between 47% and 74 % from 2001 to 2004,[63] and is not, as its name might suggest, specifically focused on the causes of conflict.[64] The Government rightly points out that,

> "in post-conflict societies, an important intervention to prevent future conflicts is the creation of effective and democratically accountable armed forces and police services. The UK has been instrumental in taking forward the SSR agenda and providing support to SSR programmes in sub-Saharan Africa."[65]

67. In the DRC we saw the inadequate living and working conditions of the newly reintegrated armed forces. We were told that inadequate provisions led the armed forces to prey on the local population, for example by compelling villagers to construct living quarters for the soldiers and their families. The very slow progress on SSR is of particular concern given the continuation of low level conflict in the east.

68. In contrast, DFID has clearly made important, painstaking progress with SSR in Sierra Leone. We were impressed by the work of the International Military Assistance and Training Team (IMATT), funded through the ACCP, and improvements in the relationship between the police and armed forces which have been achieved. We are convinced that investment in SSR has made a vital contribution to Sierra Leone's stability.

69. The International Crisis Group (ICG) has pointed out that spending on security sector reform is constrained by the DAC guidelines which restrict the use of Official Development Assistance (ODA) for military spending.[66] ICG noted that this was particularly problematic for the EU's ODA,[67] but the Secretary of State insisted that he did not believe funding of security sector reform was problematic.

---

63   OECD, *DAC Peer Review: United Kingdom*, p 20.

64   Q 6 (Oli Brown, IISD)

65   DFID, *The Africa Conflict Prevention Pool: an information document*, September 2004, p 17.

66   House of Lords EU Select Committee, *The EU and Africa: toward a strategic partnership*, 34th Report, Session 2005-6 HL 206

67   House of Lords, *ibid.* Q337

"I think we have the means in place, particularly through the Pools, that allow us to do what are, in my view, extremely sensible things to try and reduce insecurity and promote peace and stability in the interest ultimately, as far as I am concerned, of helping countries to make progress in fighting poverty."[68]

70. In fact the way in which the Pools were set up, as inter-departmental units, means that DFID can fund SSR projects which would not normally be eligible for ODA funding. Thus they free DFID from the obligation, under the 2002 International Development Act, to ensure that the primary objective of its activities is poverty alleviation. The debate about what is and what is not eligible for ODA funding according to the DAC rules is ongoing. The European Commission, for example, has been arguing with the European Parliament about how best to tackle security issues in developing countries. The European Parliament and non-governmental organisations are adamant that development money should not be used for issues such as security, crime or immigration and that these need to be funded separately by the EU.[69] Their concern is that, under the guise of a 'war on terror', development is becoming increasingly subject to the security concerns of donors. The DAC makes a distinction between governance and activities designed to strengthen security forces, the latter being non-eligible for ODA funding. The DAC has already reviewed its eligibility guidelines in 2005 and produced a list of six new areas eligible for ODA which maintain the restriction on using DAC funds to strengthen security forces.[70] We have already said that security is a prerequisite for all developmental activity. In some places an effective security force is more important than other traditional aspects of development which cannot be guaranteed without the necessary security.

71. The debate on the eligibility of funding security sector reform through ODA is not going to go away. It is important that the Government monitors and contributes to this debate. The Government will need to take a position on whether or not ODA-eligible expenditure can be extended further. While DFID has a clear policy which seeks to ensure that 90% of its funding goes to the poorest states, and the Pools facilitate expenditure on non-ODA eligible items, other EU members, and the European Commission, do not have such restrictions or the equivalent of the Pools. Given the importance of security sector reform in CPCA states this is a matter of some urgency. We believe the definition of ODA should not be expanded to include military expenditure.

68   Q 272 (Hilary Benn, DFID)

69   *European Voice* 22 June 2006.

70   The six new areas are:

-    The management of security expenditure through improved ~~~~~~~~~ ight and democratic control of budgeting, management, accountability and auditing of security expenditure.

-    Enhancing civil society's role in the security system to help ensure that it is managed in accordance with democratic norms and principles of accountability, transparency and good governance.

-    Security system reform to improve democratic governance and civilian control.

-    Supporting legislation for preventing the recruitment of child soldiers.

-    Controlling, preventing and reducing the proliferation of small arms and light weapons.

-    Civilian activities for peace-building, conflict prevention and conflict resolution.

Aprodev, *Whose Security? Integration and integrity in EU policies for security and development.* June 2005

3 Building the peace

The greed or grievance debate

72. Violent conflict is often a result of the breakdown of a society's mechanisms for dealing with change and mediating between different groups. However, conflict may serve a variety of political, social and economic functions for individuals or groups. Many actors may have a stake in the continuation of conflict. Consequently, the idea that conflict will end as soon as a peace agreement is signed is unrealistic. Building peace is a process which needs to involve not just the leaders of rebel groups and the government, but representatives of all those who are involved or caught up, in a voluntary or involuntary manner, in the conflict.

73. Building a viable peace involves addressing the causes or 'drivers' of conflict so that conflicts do not re-emerge at a later date. Some have suggested that if there are economic causes of conflict, these are usually attributable to "greed" and that such greed is normally much more significant to the conflict than any political or social grievances in the country concerned. We have no doubt that the quest for personal or corporate gain — nationally and internationally — has been a key driver of conflict and continues to be so — particularly in the exploitation of natural resources. However, we do not believe that "greed versus grievance" arguments are particularly helpful or illuminating.

Addressing grievances

74. Grievances matter — if left unresolved, they may resurface later on. Given that 50% of conflicts restart within ten years[71], it is clear that the causes of conflict must be tackled as part of peacebuilding activities. It is true that even intense grievances do not always lead to rebellion, and this is partly how extreme inequalities develop in the first place, but if the grievances which contributed to a conflict are not properly addressed, peace agreements will not last.

75. Professor Collier, one of the witnesses in our inquiry, adopts an approach which tends to minimise grievances as causal factors in conflict.[72] Based on other evidence we heard, we think that some behaviour which is labelled as greed in such an approach may in fact hide grievances. Poverty, for example, can be a grievance. What is less clear is whether the grievance is about simply being poor, or being poor while others are becoming rich. The latter would lead to questions of inequalities. There is disagreement over the role played by inequalities in generating conflict. While Professor Collier asserts that his statistical analysis does not show inequality as a strong factor in the emergence of conflict,[73] evidence from Robert Picciotto suggests that horizontal inequalities, or the exclusion of ethnic or religious groups from economic opportunities, can be a causal factor in the onset or return

---

71   Ev 204 (Peace Direct)

72   Professor Collier uses statistical analysis of the causes of conflict to argue that recent conflicts have been driven largely by greed rather than grievance. However because greed and grievance are not straightforwardly quantifiable factors Collier applies measurable proxies for each. The choice of proxies raises some questions – a heavy reliance on the export of primary commodities, used as a proxy for greed, could also be understood as an indicator of lack of development, and hence of the grievance which this often produces.

73   Q 107 (Prof Collier, University of Oxford)

to conflict.[74] It may be difficult to determine the true motivation for all actions, and hence the extent to which behaviour is motivated by greed or grievance.[75] However, if grievances are expressed as a contributing factor to the emergence or perpetuation of conflict, they must be investigated and addressed.

Challenging impunity, transitional justice

76. Transitional justice refers to a range of approaches which societies take in order to deal with the legacies of widespread human rights abuses as they move from conflict towards peace and the rule of law. The way in which each society chooses to deal with its past will differ depending on the context, and the peculiarities of the conflict. The approaches may be both judicial and non-judicial. That is, they may involve domestic or international prosecutions of perpetrators, or they may involve an approach similar to that pioneered by South Africa's Truth and Reconciliation Committee. Reparations may be required and some institutional reform may also be necessary, especially where the arms of the state have been involved in such abuses.

77. The UK Government has invested heavily in peacemaking activities in Sierra Leone since 2000. In particular, it has funded the building and running of a Special Court to put on trial the leaders of the conflict.[76] During our visit to Sierra Leone we were told, on several occasions, that the operations of the Special Court were seen by most Sierra Leoneans as unconnected to their lives and their experiences of the conflict. The Court is expensive to run at US$25 million a year; it had great difficulty in getting neighbouring countries to surrender one of the key leaders of the conflict, Charles Taylor, to stand trial (although his arrest has been widely welcomed); and has only indicted thirteen people from all sides of the conflict. There are thousands of other people responsible for crimes under international law who will not stand trial. We were unconvinced by plans we heard for the 'legacy' of the Special Court which includes building up the capacity of the justice system in Sierra Leone, and the future use of an expensive building.

78. While initiatives such as the Special Court can address some grievances, for example the abuses committed by the leaders of the conflict, a more 'bottom up' approach — listening to, and seeking to deal with the concerns of youth, the rural poor, and other groups in civil society — would be likely to produce a wider perception that grievances were being taken seriously. When we challenged DFID about the fact that in Sierra Leone people continue to live in villages with neighbours known to have committed atrocities, DFID responded that:

> "a Truth and Reconciliation Commission (TRC) was established in 2000 in Sierra Leone and presented its report to the government in 2004. It was mandated to make findings in relation to the causes, nature and extent of violations and abuses during the armed conflict. It was also mandated as part of its brief to make recommendations for implementation of a reparations programme for the victims of

---

74   Ev 146 (Prof Picciotto, Kings College, London)

75   Q 113 (Prof Collier, University of Oxford)

76   The Special Court was set up jointly by the UN and the Government of Sierra Leone at the request of the latter to try those with greatest responsibility for war crimes and crimes against humanity committed since 1996 during the Sierra Leone civil war. There are eleven persons indicted by the Special Court, www.specialcourt.org.

the conflict. The government has been very slow to address many of the report's recommendations but did decide in August that the yet to be established National Human Rights Commission should take the TRC's work forward. This Commission is currently being appointed."[77]

79. In most cases it would be almost impossible to punish or record all abuses. The process would consume huge resources, and it could be argued that such a policy runs the risk of destabilizing the newly found order. Also it is not uncommon to assume that people are either abusers or victims, when in some conflicts many have been both.[78]

80. Grievances matter because if they are not properly addressed they risk precipitating a return to conflict. It is a necessary, but not sufficient, step to address only the crimes committed by high level officials and rebel leaders. While this approach, exemplified in the Special Court of Sierra Leone, sends a message of challenging impunity, too often it only scratches the surface. Abuses and crimes carried out at a lower level also need to be addressed in a manner which recognises the impact of the conflict on communities, families and individuals. In this way peacebuilding will have greater local ownership and more chance of lasting.

Traditional justice in Uganda

81. Traditional justice refers to local or customary norms used to resolve disputes or allocate resources. On our visit to northern Uganda we met the Acholi religious and traditional leaders who have formed the Acholi Religious Leaders Peace Initiative (ARLPI). They, along with some civil society groups we met, expressed a desire for a negotiated settlement with the LRA. Their view is that the Government of Uganda has expended a great deal of effort and resources on a military solution to the conflict with little success and has not tried to negotiate seriously with the LRA. When a negotiated peace settlement was closest, the ARLPI claim that the Government of Uganda imposed a tight deadline for signing the agreement, one which would have been impossible for the LRA to meet. The ARLPI base their approach on the concept of justice held by many Acholi which allows for forgiveness and reconciliation. They argue that it is the Acholi people who should be directing the pace and content of a peace agreement.

82. In October 2005 the referral of the case of northern Uganda to the International Criminal Court (ICC) by President Museveni resulted in the first arrest warrants, which have met with mixed support in Uganda. Evidence we received from Christian Aid and from the Northern Uganda Advocacy Partnership for Peace (NUAPP) expressed concern about the sequencing of ICC investigations and possible prosecutions. Christian Aid contend that while the ICC has an important role to play in ending the culture of impunity, if badly managed its involvement could prolong and intensify the violence. ICC engagement alone will not end the conflict, and if the international community is serious in its desire for peace it should also be supporting mediation, the reintegration of combatants and plans for reconstruction.[79] We agree. We gained the impression that

---

77   Ev 122 (DFID)

78   David Keen, *Conflict and Collusion in Sierra Leone,* Oxford: James Curry, 2005.

79   Ev 170 (Christian Aid)

Uganda's Amnesty Commission was working well and that initiatives to reintegrate abducted people had recognised that one person can be both a victim and a perpetrator. Most of these initiatives were funded by donors, but there is an obvious need for the Government of Uganda to be seen to be involved in such processes, especially as the north has been an area of political opposition to Museveni's Government.

83. It was put to us that the Acholi people exhibit a remarkable capacity to forgive those who may have committed atrocities against their own communities, especially (and perhaps most understandably) children. At the Amnesty Commission Office in Gulu we met three children who had been abducted by the LRA and subsequently had returned to their families and communities. We also visited a Reception Centre for returning child combatants, including young women with children born as a result of rape by the LRA. They were being cared for, and demobilised, before being sent back to their communities. At the same time, people we spoke to in IDP camps expressed a deep fear of the LRA, and a desire not to leave the camps until they were certain it was safe to do so. The Government of Uganda is unable to guarantee their security or to effect a military solution. The issuing of ICC warrants for the arrest of the top five leaders of the LRA provides an opportunity to ensure that impunity is ended, at least for the leadership of the LRA, and does not foreclose local attempts at reconciliation and the use of traditional justice.[80] Recent offers of amnesty to the leadership of the LRA by the Government of Uganda present a dilemma, as this could undermine the credibility of the ICC, whose reputation may also be damaged if pressing for the full implementation of the indictments was the only obstacle to a peace agreement which would allow people to return to their homes.

84. Traditional justice in Uganda offers an important opportunity to recognise local norms and customs, and a means of ensuring that such justice is bottom-up and locally owned. Despite fears expressed by some CSOs we support the issuing of ICC warrants for the leadership of the LRA. We are concerned at the recent offer of amnesty to the leadership of the LRA by the Government of Uganda. The ICC is an international initiative to end impunity for serious war crimes. We hope that the UK Government, a founding member of the ICC, will help to ensure that the credibility of the organisation is not damaged by the actions of the Government of Uganda.

Governance: the role and timing of elections

85. It has come to be expected that soon after the signing of a peace accord, an electoral process should be set up or re-established, and (ideally) multiparty elections held within a short period of time. Elections provide an important opportunity to engage the whole population, victims and perpetrators, in an acceptance of the peace process and the conferring of legitimacy on its outcomes. In addition, an elected government should provide the necessary channels for the electorate to voice their grievances and find collective solutions for these. The example of Uganda's recent elections demonstrates some of the issues surrounding donor support for elections.

---

80   For more discussion of traditional justice in Uganda see, Tim Allen, *Trial Justice: the ICC and the LRA*, London: Zed Books 2006.

86. Uganda held its first multi-party elections in 2006. The elections themselves received a clean bill of health from international election monitors. However the process leading up to the elections did give rise to some concerns from the UK Government, and later other donors. In May 2005 the UK Government withheld £5 million of its £40 million budget support for 2005–06 to the Government of Uganda because "insufficient progress had been made towards establishing a fair basis for a multi-party system".[81] In December 2005 the UK Government withheld £15 million from the 2006–07 allocation because of delays in putting in place the procedures for multiparty elections, the continued use of state funds for Museveni's own party and the arrest of the leader of the opposition, Kizza Besigye. We have already commented on the seeming confusion in the UK Government's approach to issues of governance and issues of conflict. A further concern is that international donors have held up Uganda, and Museveni's Government, as an example of good development practice, but have not devised a development strategy short of the blunt instrument of withholding funds which conflicts with another DFID objective – predictability of aid.

87. The ODI, in a paper written by Paolo de Renzio, calls the UK response to Museveni's actions prior to the elections a late reaction to a foreseeable event.[82] He argues for greater historical analysis, more joint action with other donors and, importantly, the development of domestic accountability institutions – for example an independent Parliament, think tanks, and civil society organisations which provide an effective counterbalance to the government. **We agree with the ODI that the building up of institutions for democratic accountability should play a larger role in donor governments' support for electoral processes. It would also bring an end to the practice of adopting 'donor darlings' based on personalities rather than conduct and the strength of institutions. This would allow for peaceful transition between rulers and eliminate the perpetuation of one person rule or elites.**

88. In the DRC we saw much international effort being put into the holding of elections in July 2006. The UK Government played a significant role in facilitating the process. We met the head of the Election Commission in Kinshasa who explained to us the challenges of organising an election in a country as large as the DRC with most places outside Kinshasa being inaccessible by road. The UN Peacekeeping force, MONUC, helped to drop and collect electoral material in remote areas. The turnout on the day was high and the elections were largely peaceful.

89. The political parties fighting the election in the DRC reflect many of the factional lines of the former conflict in the country. In the event of the losers not accepting the result or the victors using their victory to deny losers a say in subsequent governance arrangements, there is clearly the danger of armed conflict breaking out once again. In the first round of the DRC presidential elections Joseph Kabila's support came largely from the east and Jean-Pierre Bemba's from the west of the country. It is important that the winner of the second round ballot, on 29 October, includes leaders from all parts of the country in the government.

---

81   Ev 190 (Northern Uganda Advocacy Partnership for Peace)

82   Paolo de Renzio, *The primacy of domestic politics and the dilemmas of aid: what can donors do in Ethiopia and Uganda?* www.odi.org.uk February 2006.

90. Some commentators have voiced concerns about the tendency to rush towards elections in countries emerging from conflict, often as part of the peace agreement. Paul Collier argues that elections do not reduce the risk of conflict, they simply shift it to the future.[83] Evidence from International Alert for example reports that rushed elections can sometimes fuel instability.[84] In his book, *At War's End*, Roland Paris argues that the international community is seeking to create liberal democratic systems in post-conflict countries before the appropriate institutional preconditions and safeguards are in place.[85]

91. Paris identifies two key preconditions for peaceful and successful elections. These are: firstly, that there should be an adequate security force, local or international, capable of maintaining basic security; and secondly, that there are electoral rules and mechanisms in place for dealing with the disputes over the outcome of the elections. In addition, he argues that where there are armed factions capable of disrupting the process and overturning the outcome, demobilisation and disarmament may be another precondition.[86] What is needed, Paris argues, is not quick elections but a greater focus on the building up of governmental institutions which can manage political and economic reforms. DFID recognises this to some degree, although a significant part of its budget in the DRC has nevertheless been allocated to supporting the electoral process. DFID officials told us that they were unable to think of any alternative to elections to deal with the post-conflict situation in DRC.[87]

92. **Institution-building in post-conflict societies is a crucial part of improving governance. Democratic elections are essential for creating a legitimate government. The establishment of a democratic system is a long-term project, which must be owned by the people. Donors should not suppose that one free multi-party election will entrench democracy. Long-term aid will continue to be needed in post-conflict states to build and strengthen accountable institutions and to nurture a democratic culture.**

The economic dimension of conflict

The regional dimension of conflict

93. We have been told that the regional dimension of conflict is often neglected by policy makers.[88] One of our witnesses, Dr Cooper, of the Department of Peace Studies, University of Bradford, argues that development and post-conflict reconstruction policies underestimate the interconnections — political, economic, military and social — across borders which characterise many conflicts. One consequence of ignoring regional linkages is that the imposition of a regulatory framework in one state may simply have the unintended consequence of shifting problems such as trafficking, weapons proliferation,

---

83 Q 127 (Prof Collier, University of Oxford)

84 Ev 181 (International Alert)

85 Roland Paris, *At wars end: building peace after civil conflict*, Cambridge University Press ,2004.

86 Toward more effective Peacebuilding: a conversation with Roland Paris, *Development in Practice*, vol 15, no 6, November 2005.

87 International Development Committee, DFID Departmental Report 2006, Unprinted oral evidence Q 27 (Ms Shafik) HC-1491-i

88 Q 213 (Dr Cooper, University of Bradford)

and even conflict, across borders. Dr Cooper explained to us how West Africa and the Mano River Union sub-region offer a perfect example of regional mercenary activity:

> "What you have had is that a group of mercenaries have moved around from conflict to conflict and have been part of the problem. It seems to me that simply launching nationally-based DDR[89] programmes does not address that problem totally. At some level you need a regional focus to think through the fact that you have got this group of actors who are moving across borders, and who are not the only reason which is bringing about conflicts but they are part of a set of factors which are facilitating the next conflict which is going to happen next-door."[90]

94. Our visit to the DRC illustrated to us the need for a regional approach to peacebuilding in the Great Lakes region. The UN Office for the Co-ordination of Humanitarian Affairs (UN-OCHA) estimates that the conflict has created over 1.7 million internally displaced persons and over 300,000 refugees in neighbouring countries. In addition there is continuing hostility by external armed groups such as the Forces Démocratique de Libération du Rwanda (FDLR) in North and South Kivu, and other rebel groups operating further north in the Ituri region which borders Uganda and Sudan.

95. DFID funds a number of regional and sub-regional organisations through the Africa Conflict Prevention Pool. Since 2003 the Africa Pool has also been used to fund DFID's regional conflict advisers, four of whom are now based in Africa. It is too early to evaluate the efforts of these regional advisers but we were struck by the fact that in Sierra Leone, MoD advisers working with the Sierra Leone armed forces told us that they were unaware of the activities of the West African regional conflict adviser, even though these advisers are supposed to report jointly to DFID, MoD and the FCO. DFID did not provide evidence of any mechanisms for communication and we felt this indicated a deficit in communication between two key players, DFID and MoD. Moreover, these advisers are there not so much to provide a regional analysis of conflict as to provide conflict analysis, on a regional basis, to assist in the formation of country strategies.[91] **We accept that DFID may not be able to place conflict advisers in all conflict settings; consequently the role of regional advisers is even more significant. DFID therefore needs to ensure that regional advisers are visible, and communicating regularly with all branches of the UK Government.**

96. **Conflicts, the effects of conflict, and the people who wage them, do not always recognize state borders. The building up of trans-national capacities in Africa through the Africa Conflict Prevention Pools is, in our view, the right approach in that it promises to facilitate greater regional ownership of peacebuilding policies. But donors should also give serious consideration to carrying out, if possible jointly, regional conflict analyses as part of their approach to conflict, so that they do not solely succeed in moving problems from one state to the next.**

---

89   Disarmament, Demobilization and Reintegration

90   Q 213 (Dr Cooper, University of Bradford)

91   Ev 108 (DFID)

Managing natural resource wealth

97. Natural resource exploitation has played an increasingly prominent role in conflicts around the world since the end of the Cold War. According to the International Institute for Sustainable Development:

> "The presence of some commodities, particularly oil, may make the initiation of conflict more likely; the presence of others, for example gemstones and narcotics, may lengthen the duration of conflicts. Revenues and riches may alter the mindset of combatants, turning war and insurgency from a purely political activity to an economic one; conflicts become less about grievance and more about greed."[92]

98. The focus on the role of natural resource wealth rather than scarcity as a cause of armed conflict has provided a new explanatory framework for conflict analysis. In particular, it suggests that there is a larger role for trade and trade policy as an integral part of donor approaches to CPCA states. It also points towards the important role which donor trade and investment policies can play as part of an overall conflict policy.

99. Paul Collier described what he saw as three economic components which increased the risk of conflict: low income, low growth and natural resources. If a country had all three, he said, the chances of conflict occurring were extremely high.[93] However, the link between natural resources and conflict depends critically on the ability of their exploiters to access external markets. If you take away the ability to earn returns from resource extraction, their value to the promoters of conflict falls away.[94]

100. There are various methods by which this can be done. One way to exclude natural resources associated with conflict from international markets is through the use of sanctions. DFID maintains that sanctions can play a role in addressing the issue of conflict resources, primarily by placing restrictions on the export of certain commodities which are being used to fund arms purchases.[95] However, blanket restrictions on trade do not work if conflict resources can be smuggled into neighbouring countries, or if the economic and social development of a country depends on the legitimate exploitation of the resources in question. A more targeted solution is to develop systems to identify and license resources produced legally. The Kimberley Process for diamonds is one example of international action which has created a two-tier market of legitimately and illegitimately-sourced diamonds. The idea is to squeeze the finances of rebel movements while the conflict continues by only permitting trade in certified diamonds.

101. The Kimberley Process works well but is not without its problems.[96] It would be unwieldy to create the equivalent of the Kimberley Process for every category of resources which might be used to fund conflict. Many NGOs agree with the Commission for Africa's recommendation that a more effective solution would be for the UN to agree a definition

---

92 Ev 144 (IISD)

93 Q 102 (Prof Collier, University of Oxford)

94 Ev 144 (IISD)

95 Ev 110 (DFID)

96 See *Global Witness, Making it Work: why the Kimberley process must do more to stop conflict diamonds,* November 2005.

of 'conflict resources' which would assist the international community in differentiating between natural resources used to fund conflict legitimately, and natural resource extraction and trade used to fund illegitimate activities, which may contribute to the violation of human rights. They argue that such a definition could help prevent and manage conflict.[97] The Commission for Africa also recommended the creation of a UN Expert Panel to monitor links between natural resource extraction and violent conflict.[98] The Government has told us that negotiating an agreed definition of conflict resources through the UN Security Council will be difficult, although they are discussing how to move this forward, together with the creation of an Expert Panel to monitor conflict resources. A cross-Whitehall working group on natural resources and conflict has recently been formed to coordinate government policy on this issue.[99]

102. In our view, the Government needs, as a matter of urgency, to take forward the Commission for Africa's recommendation of a definition of conflict resources, and an Expert Panel in the UN Security Council. Without an agreed definition the international community's approach will continue to be piecemeal, ad hoc and inconsistent. An internationally agreed definition of conflict resources would make it unnecessary to have a 'Kimberley Process' for every resource.

Corporate Social Responsibility and the DRC

103. Investment by international businesses in CPCA states is usually welcomed by those with an interest in development as an indication that business sees the environment as sufficiently stable and predictable to ensure a positive return on investments. In fact, the reverse is often the case. Foreign companies may seek investments, or continue to invest, in CPCA countries precisely because they can take advantage of instability and of weak and ineffective government regulation. This has been the case with easily extractable and valuable resources such as those found in eastern DRC: coltan, cassiterite, timber, gold, and diamonds. This does not mean that foreign investment should be discouraged in such countries but it does mean that natural resource trade in CPCA states should be approached in a way which recognises the potential contribution of natural resource wealth to the onset and continuation of conflict.

104. Demands for greater corporate responsibility have increased in the last two decades. Many companies have responded to criticism of their activities by developing Corporate Social Responsibility (CSR) codes. NGOs such as ActionAid have criticised the voluntary nature of these codes arguing that they result in insufficient standards of protection for human rights and the environment.[100] Many civil society organisations support stronger regulation of corporate behaviour through, for example, the OECD Guidelines for Multinational Enterprises. These guidelines provide companies with a set of recommendations on good corporate behaviour. The UK Government view, which has

---

97   Ev 139 (Global Witness)

98   Commission for Africa, *Our Common Interest*, p 174.

99   Ev 120 (DFID)

100 International Development Committee, Fourth Report of Session 2005-6, *Private Sector Development* HC 921 para 157

been discussed in our report on *Private Sector Development*,[101] is that a voluntary approach to regulation is adequate at present. The following section explores the operation of the OECD Guidelines in the DRC and considers the limitations of this approach in situations of conflict.

The UN panel on the illegal exploitation of natural resources in the DRC

105. In June 2000, the UN Security Council asked the Secretary General to create an expert panel to investigate the exploitation of natural resources in the DRC. The first report of the panel (April 2001) concluded that: "conflict in the DRC has become mainly about access, control and trade of five key mineral resources: coltan, diamonds, copper, cobalt and gold." In addition, it states that:

> "the role of the private sector in the exploitation of natural resources and the continuation of the war has been vital. A number of companies have been involved and have fuelled the war directly, trading arms for natural resources. Others have facilitated access to financial resources, which are used to purchase weapons. Companies trading minerals, which the Panel considered to be 'the engine of the conflict in the DRC' have prepared the field for illegal mining activities in the country." [102]

The report recommended an extended mandate for the panel and a follow-up investigation.

106. In October 2002 a second report was published. Annex III of this report listed 85 businesses operating in violation of OECD Guidelines, including 12 UK companies. The list provoked a strong reaction in business and political circles. Most companies thought the UN panel process was problematic. Companies were not consulted before they were listed, and there have been accusations that the allegations were opaque and unsubstantiated.[103]

107. A third report was published in October 2003 whose purpose was to "verify, reinforce and update its earlier findings and, as necessary, revise the annexes attached to its previous report". To do this it attempted to pursue "dialogue with individuals, companies and states referred to in the report, exchange information with those parties, assess actions taken by them and compile their reactions for publication as an attachment to the report."[104] The Panel stressed that it was not a judicial body and that its mandate precluded it from determining guilt or innocence, so instead it had focused on "identifying parties where it has information indicating a *prima facie* case to answer", either regarding illegal activity or the "breach of international norms of corporate governance and ethics". The Panel sought to achieve a resolution of the issues which led companies to be listed in the annexes. This was not always possible and consequently five different categories of subsequent outcomes

---

101 International Development Committee *ibid*

102 UN, *UN Expert Panel on the illegal exploitation of natural resources and other forms of wealth in the DRC*, April 2001 report S/2001/357. p 41

103 Discussion with UK National Contact Point.

104 Final report of the *UN expert panel on the illegal exploitation of natural resources and other forms of wealth in the DRC*, October 2003. S/2003/1027

were established. Most companies were either directly or indirectly listed as resolved, while some were referred to their National Contact Points (NCP) for further investigation.[105] Four UK companies are recommended by the Panel for further investigation by the UK National Contact Point. Three of these have been investigated and the outstanding company, Das Air, is in the process of being investigated with the NGO Rights and Accountability in Development (RAID) as the complainant.

108. Some NGOs criticised the final report which listed the majority of companies as 'resolved', despite the fact in some cases *prima facie* issues of misconduct had been identified. The UN Panel report had stated that resolved did not mean absolved, nor did it invalidate earlier findings.[106] NGOs therefore felt that 'closure' could only occur once NCPs had examined the conduct of all companies mentioned, including those deemed resolved.[107]

109. We do not propose to examine in detail here the manner in which the UK NCP carried out its investigations of the four UK companies. The All Party Parliamentary Group on the Great Lakes region of Africa has carried out such research and established a Joint Working Group (JWG), which includes businesses and NGOs, to explore the scope for common ground and to establish frameworks for business conduct in areas of conflict and weak governance. The JWG produced guidelines for the reform of the UK NCP in response to a the DTI consultation.[108] Many of their suggestions have been incorporated into the revised operating procedures for the NCP including making the NCP a jointly-owned body between the DTI, FCO, and DFID.[109] **We believe that the Joint Working Group guidelines have contributed to major improvements in the operation of the UK's National Contact Point.**

110. We are concerned with the manner in which companies, some UK-based, were put in the resolved category by the UN Panel. For example, Afrimex, a company trading coltan and cassiterite from North and South Kivu, was put into the resolved category by the UN after a meeting with them. When Global Witness carried out research in eastern DRC in February 2005, Afrimex was the second largest recipient of cassiterite from the province of South Kivu. Official Congolese export documents reveal that in 2004 and early 2005, Afrimex purchased large quantities of cassiterite, and a smaller quantity of coltan, from two traders in South Kivu — Muyeye and Olive. The value of this cassiterite amounted to US$1,308,000 in 2004, which is 42.95% of the total cassiterite exported officially from South Kivu in that year. According to staff in the office of Société Kotecha in Bukavu, this ore came from all parts of South Kivu province and Walikale, in North Kivu province, where various militias were still fighting to control the mines throughout 2004. Minerals

---

105 Under OECD Guidelines, adhering countries are required to establish a National Contact Point (NCP) to handle inquiries and discuss with concerned parties all matters covered by the Guidelines. The role of the NCP is two-fold, to promote the Guidelines and also to contribute to the resolution of issues that arise relating to their implementation.

106 UN, *Third UN Panel Report on the illegal exploitation of natural resources and other forms of wealth from the DRC*, October 2003, S/2003/1027, para 23.

107 See, for example, Christian Aid, *Flagship or failure?*

108 DTI, Review of the Functioning of OECD Guidelines for MNCs.

109 DFID, *Making governance work for the poor*, p 36

could not be taken out of many of these mines without payments being made to the controlling militias.

111. By early 2005, the Congolese army had gained control over Bisie mine in Walikale, the largest cassiterite mine in North Kivu. However, we have been told that government troops have continued to commit abuses at the mine and there are reports of soldiers using forced labour to mine and carry the cassiterite.[110]

112. Afrimex stated that they had been operating in the DRC since 1962 and that they had invested heavily in the country.[111] They had maintained their investments and trading activities throughout the conflict. Mr Kotecha, the Managing Director, told us that he had not changed his operations as a result of the conflict, but had simply paid taxes to the authorities in South Kivu during the conflict —to the RCD-Goma — a Rwandan-backed militia group.[112] We were shown a copy of a letter which was sent from a military commander in the RCD-Goma to businesses in South Kivu offering protection in return for financial assistance.

113. Mr Kotecha also insisted that he had no knowledge of OECD guidelines, nor had he ever been contacted by the UK NCP or the British Embassy in Kinshasa after his company had been named in the UN Panel Report.[113] In a subsequent letter to the Committee, Mr Kotecha sought to draw a line between the activities of Afrimex UK and those of the Société Kotecha in Bukavu.[114]

114. We also heard evidence from RAID about the activities of another British company, Alfred Knight, which provides assaying services for minerals from the DRC, and in particular from mines which dealt with minerals coming from mines in the Kivus which were under rebel control, and where it was known that human rights abuses were being committed.[115] RAID showed us a document from a German company which stated that they had secured the services of Alfred Knight to operate their laboratory facilities in Rwanda and Mozambique. This German company, Karl Heinz Albers, was also listed in the UN Panel Report.[116]

115. Alfred Knight did not accept our invitation to give evidence to the Committee. In a letter to us they wrote that they "often work at arm's length with no real knowledge of the origin of any particular sample being analysed."[117] Despite the company having being named, and subsequently deemed resolved by the UN Panel, RAID are concerned that the process did not result in any change in its activities and that Alfred Knight may still be providing assaying services for minerals from conflict-affected areas of the DRC.[118]

---

110 See Channel 4's news report, 'Tin Soldiers', broadcast 30 June 2005·

111 Ev 135, Letter from Mr Kotecha to the UN Expert Panel

112 Q 391-94, 426, 428 (Mr Kotecha, Afrimex)

113 Q 415 and 422-24 (Mr Kotecha, Afrimex)

114 Ev 135

115 Q 365-367 (Ms Feeney, RAID)

116 Q 367 (Ms Feeney, RAID), Ev 240 (AHK)

117 Letter from Alfred Knight, 22 June 2006, placed in library and Ev 240 (AHK)

118 Q 34-7 (Ms Feeney, RAID)

116. The UK Government has not sought to pursue investigations into the activities of Alfred Knight even though RAID told us they had sent information to the Crown Prosecution Service in 2004, to the Metropolitan Police, and to DTI's Companies Investigative Branch.[119] We have subsequently received written evidence from Thomas Eggenburg of the Krall Metal company in the DRC which alleges that Alfred Knight is involved in activities which contribute to the fuelling of war in the DRC.[120] Mr Eggenburg states that Alfred Knight plays a key role in the rare metal business in the DRC and that their assaying services are key in determining the purchase price of minerals such as coltan.[121] In addition, he maintains that if Alfred Knight had refused to provide its assaying services to coltan from the DRC the coltan mining business in the DRC would have collapsed. Subsequent to our evidence session we also received written evidence from Alfred Knight which seeks to explain their role in the DRC and states that they have not been in violation of OECD guidelines.[122] We are not in a position to verify the claims of either of these companies. However they do raise concerns about the UN process of putting companies into the 'resolved' category, and about how vigorously the UK seeks to ensure that OECD guidelines are adhered to by British companies operating in conflict zones. **We are surprised and disappointed that the DTI did not contact Afrimex about their activities or investigate the activities of Alfred Knight in relation to the DRC. We believe the DTI could do more to promote the EITI and to resolve issues surrounding conflict resources.**

117. **There is a serious deficiency in the manner in which the Government approaches the actions of UK companies abroad, and in particular in CPCA countries. The Government does not send out a strong message to UK companies about the significance it attaches to OECD Guidelines. Given the number of UK companies originally listed by the UN and, given the human rights abuses which we know accompanied the war, and continue to be perpetrated, the Government response should have been more thorough. The Government needs to demonstrate that it takes the OECD guidelines seriously, in practice as well as in theory, by drawing up practical measures to ensure their implementation.**

118. The OECD has now produced a *Risk Awareness Tool for Multinational Enterprises in Weak Governance Zones*[123] in order to raise awareness of the risks of operating in weak governance zones and to offer companies some guidelines. This OECD initiative was given backing by the G8 in 2005 in the Gleneagles Summit Communiqué. The OECD Council recommends "the widest possible dissemination of the Risk Awareness Tool and its active use."[124]

---

119 Q 3-49 (MS Feeney, RAID)

120 Ev 241 Supporting documents placed in library.

121 Ev 249 (Krall Métal, DRC)

122 Ev 230-241 (Alfred Knight)

123 OECD, *Risk Awareness Tool for MNEs in weak governance zones*. OECD, 2006

124 OECD, *Risk Awareness Tool for MNEs in weak governance zones*. OECD, 2006.

119. **Tools are of little use if they do not change behaviour.** If Afrimex has not been made aware of OECD guidelines by the DTI, and appears to have had no interest in making themselves aware of them, there may be other British companies operating in zones of weak governance who are also unaware of OECD guidelines. These may not be the large household-name companies who cannot risk bad publicity. Such companies often will not operate in CPCA states. But it cannot be assumed that improved conduct will trickle down from socially conscious companies to the poor performers.[125] **The Government has a responsibility to make UK Companies aware of the OECD guidelines and to offer them appropriate advice. There is a pressing need for the UK Government to consider ways to ensure that the approach of the DTI is not at odds with other aspects of Government policy in CPCA states. Without such coherence the Government cannot hope to have the impact it seeks through DFID's new strategy of engagement in fragile states. We intend to take evidence from DTI ministers on these important issues.**

Transforming war economies

120. The transition from war to peace and the brokering of a peace agreement is not usually characterised by a definite end to fighting, or to the economies of warfare. Instead there is often a long transition process in which economic strategies and political alignments must be adjusted to the new exigencies of peace, including addressing exclusion and deprivation. Reform of both the security and justice sectors is thus an important objective for peacebuilding interventions. The effectiveness of strategies designed to effect such reforms depends crucially on an understanding of the reasons for the conflict and the motivations of the actors who have kept the conflict going. If these are not addressed, it will be difficult to persuade people to put down their arms and buy into the peace process. Acknowledgement of the transitional nature of peace processes entails a need to address the wide range of incentives, justifications, and reasons which cause people to engage in, and perpetuate war. In short it demands an acknowledgement of both the grievance and greed dimensions of conflict.[126]

Security Sector Reform

121. Security Sector Reform is an important means of strengthening the state and of helping to counter exclusion and deprivation by enhancing people's access to security and justice.[127] In its evidence DFID says that effective peacebuilding encompasses a wide range of security, political, social and economic initiatives including security sector reform (SSR) and demobilisation, disarmament and reintegration (DDR).[128] DFID also states that it is committed to further increasing its assistance to justice and security sector reform, and is currently leading a process within the OECD's Development Assistance Committee to

---

125   Ev 144 (IISD)

126   Pugh, Cooper and Goodhand for example propose a taxonomy of combat, shadow and coping economies to suggest various motives for, and dynamics in, waging war, profiteering and coping. See, *War Economies in a regional context*, Boulder: Lynne Rienner 2004. p. 8

127   Ev 148 (Prof Picciotto, King's College, London)

128   Ev 110 (DFID)

develop international guidance on how to implement programmes in the security and justice sector.[129]

122. We visited the prison in Bukavu on our visit to eastern DRC. The living conditions in the prison were unsatisfactory — there was evidence that the governor was not spending his budget on food for the prisoners: instead they were reliant on family and friends to bring them meals or food supplies. There was also evidence of torture. The administration of the prison was highly unsatisfactory — the prison records had been lost in a fire and were slowly being recovered; prisoners were being held on remand for long periods and only being made aware of when their case was due to be heard after payment of a fee. We were struck by the vulnerability of prisoners, even those who should be locked up, in conflict situations. **We think that the UN Peacekeeping Force in the DRC should be providing some oversight of prison conditions as part of its mandate to "facilitate humanitarian assistance and human rights monitoring, with particular attention to vulnerable groups".[130] It should also consider putting in place effective human rights monitors for prisons**.

123. On our visit to the DRC we were told about the slow pace at which the security sector reform was proceeding. An International Crisis Group report published earlier in the year had identified security sector reform in the DRC as a neglected area of donor concern.[131] The report pointed out that while generous amounts of funding had been found for demobilisation of ex-combatants, only a small fraction has gone toward improving the status and management of the armed forces and the police.[132]

124. The Transitional Government in the DRC was seeking to create a unified army out of previously distinct brigades with independent chains of command. Of a total of eighteen brigades, only six had so far been reintegrated, which involved only 45 days' training. Six more had been re-trained but could not be deployed because there was no funding or transport to move them to where they were to be stationed. There were also problems with soldiers' salaries, uniforms and housing. Salaries, themselves very low, were often paid late, some brigades did not have full uniforms and so continued to wear the uniforms from their old brigades. Very little accommodation was provided for the brigade stationed in Bukavu. The incentives to remain a solider in the newly-integrated army were few. In contrast the incentives to prey on the local population were many. This is in part because of a policy of '*brassage*' under which the newly integrated brigades had deliberately been mixed up (ethnically and tribally) and moved away from their home villages. The aim was to move soldiers away from ties which might compromise the impartiality of the army, but the consequence was that the soldiers feel no compulsion to defend or protect the local populations.

125. Many armed groups continue to operate in the DRC. The national army, the FARDC, is supposed to work alongside the UN force, MONUC, against such groups. We were told

---

129 Ev 112 (DFID)

130 Security Council Resolution 1291 of 24 February 2000 on the United Nations Organization Mission in the DRCwww.un.org.

131 International Crisis Group, *Security Sector Reform in the Congo*, 13 February 2006

132 International Crisis Group, *ibid.*

that often MONUC had simply displaced these armed groups and caused greater instability. There was an increasing recognition that such joint operations were not working. The ICG report expressed some concern that the Transitional Government in the DRC was not fully behind security sector reform because some of the leaders wanted to maintain their armed factions.

126. There was some feeling among the donor community in the DRC that the EU, rather than MONUC, should lead efforts in security sector reform. The EU had begun a valuable Chain of Payments project to help ensure that soldiers received their salaries. We were impressed by the detailed knowledge and expertise of EUSEC representatives in Kinshasa. **EU work on the Chain of Payments is an important step in the right direction, but, given the extent of insecurity in the DRC, it is a drop in the ocean. If security sector reform is to be successful in the DRC, a much larger sum of money will need to be found. The newly-elected Government of the DRC will have primary responsibility for this, but it cannot achieve this without outside assistance. Security is the basic precondition for development to take place. In our view, the UK Government needs to press the EU and its member states to make security sector reform a priority. The newly-elected government in the DRC will also need to be encouraged to make this a priority area.**

Disarmament, demobilisation and reintegration

127. The integrated nature of security and development means that material improvements are a necessary component of both post-war reconstruction and peacebuilding. Combatants and communities affected by the violence must see economic improvements which provide tangible evidence of a peace dividend. In particular, the presence of large numbers of demobilized combatants poses a security risk which can derail reconstruction. Former combatants must be shown that peace is economically advantageous in order to stave off 'spoiler' violence or organized banditry. Demobilization, disarmament, and reintegration (DDR) programmes are key to this process.[133]

128. The record of donor commitment to DDR programmes across different countries is mixed. For example in the DRC the pay-out for soldiers who disarm is quite high — US$410 — while soldiers who remain in the army are only paid US$10 per month.[134] In Uganda, in contrast, we were told that returning LRA soldiers receive very little from the Government or donors and that this was a disincentive for soldiers, who may themselves have been abducted, to come out of the bush. Retraining and re-integration programmes are now under active consideration. The relatively large sum of money received by ex-soldiers in the DRC provided a perverse incentive for them to take the payment and use the money to purchase another weapon with which they could rejoin a militia group. While the content of DDR programmes will vary in different contexts, the underlying principle must be to ensure that there are sufficient incentives and opportunities for ex-soldiers to disarm permanently and pursue civilian employment. This is a process which should not

---

133 Ev 157 (Sultan Barakat, University of York)

134 International Crisis Group, *Security sector reform in the Congo*. We have been told that the soldiers' salary is now US$20.

end with the payment for disarming, but should be linked to longer-term employment opportunities.

129. Our experience in Sierra Leone presents a good example of how this reintegration aspect of DDR is often neglected by donors. Apart from a one-off payment in cash or kind, there is not much emphasis on long-term projects to create employment for those who might otherwise pick up or return to arms. In Sierra Leone we saw first hand the large number of unemployed young men with few job prospects. Much of what we heard during our visit convinced us that one of the most significant issues facing Sierra Leone, one with the potential to contribute to future conflict, is youth unemployment. We heard that donors had invested in skills-building programmes for young people (carpentry, brick-laying etc.) without giving sufficient thought to the availability of jobs for those who have undertaken such training. **It seems clear that donors in Sierra Leone now need to give priority to employment-generation initiatives, including agricultural schemes, to provide an incentive for rural-urban migrants to return to rural areas. This will mean simultaneously tackling some of the local governance grievances that have led to discontent in rural areas.** At present a substantial proportion of unemployed young men are tempted to try their luck in the diamond mines, rather than invest their energies in gaining more secure, longer-term employment. **It may not be appropriate for DFID to engage in this area directly, but as the largest donor in Sierra Leone, the Department ought to provide a lead for other agencies by highlighting the issue and encouraging others to increase their focus on the issue.**

4 The global peacebuilding effort

Donor coordination

130. Effective action on peacebuilding and post-conflict reconstruction requires coordination and coherence among a myriad of donors and other actors including the UN and its agencies, the IMF and the World Bank, regional and sub-regional organisations, NGOs and the private sector. As well as coherence among donors it is important that donors support local initiatives by aligning objectives, programmes and processes with those of the developing country.[135]

131. Donor coherence is difficult to achieve in those countries where there is no lead donor. DFID intends to become more involved in fragile states where risks are high. These risks are increased if donor engagement is not coordinated. On our visit to the DRC we found that the small donor community operating there was not very well coordinated despite meeting regularly. At a meeting with ambassadors of donor countries we were repeatedly told this was a problem, but when we asked why nothing was being done about it we were told that the DRC was a large country with many problems and as a result finding a donor willing to take on a leading role was difficult. The European Commission seemed to us to be in a strong position to lead on donor coordination in this case, perhaps in co-operation with the USA. DFID acknowledges that donor harmonisation in the DRC has been relatively poor and that a more coordinated international community approach will be vital in the aftermath of the July elections.[136] **Because fragile states are such difficult environments in which to work, donor coordination is particularly important. In the DRC it will be vital for progress. As the largest bilateral donor, the UK Government must continue its efforts at donor harmonisation. We consider that the European Commission is best placed to take the lead on donor coordination in the DRC.**

Women and Peacebuilding

132. UN Security Council Resolution (UNSCR) 1325 on Women, Peace and Security, was adopted by the Security Council in October 2000. The Resolution recognises the disproportionate effect which conflict has on women, and underlines the essential role of women in the prevention of conflict and as full participants in post-conflict peacebuilding and reconstruction. It proposes that gender considerations should be thoroughly integrated into all aspects of UN and member states' security work, from conflict prevention to post-conflict reconstruction. This should involve:

> "increasing the participation of women in conflict resolution and peace processes; incorporating gender perspectives in peacekeeping operations and in the training of peacekeepers; taking special measures to protect women and girls from gender-based

---

135 Q 162 (Prof Picciotto, Kings College, London)

136 DFID, Overview of DFID briefing for the International Development Committee's visit to the DRC, May 2006.

violence; taking into account, in planning for disarmament, demobilisation and reintegration, the different needs of male and female ex-combatants."[137]

133. The UN Secretary-General's report of 13 October 2004, on the implementation of UNSCR 1325, requested that Member States develop their own National Action Plans for implementation. The UK Government announced its Action Plan in March 2006. This recognises the disproportionate effect of conflict on women and girls. In response to questions about specific actions various Departments had taken as a result of UNSCR 1325, DFID witnesses told us they "had a team working in DFID which is going to produce an updated 'How to' guide on gender, peace and security which we shall then bring to bear on the work we do." Phil Evans, Head of the Africa, Conflict and Humanitarian Unit, also told us about the work DFID is undertaking in Sudan to increase the involvement of women in the peacebuilding effort. [138] Despite this, on our visits to Sierra Leone, Uganda and the DRC we did not see any strong evidence that UNSCR 1325 was driving DFID's work in these conflict affected countries.

134. While we welcome the adoption of an action plan by the UK Government, we are concerned about the extent to which all Departments have 'bought-in' to the plan. We were told, in writing, that training for British military personnel being stationed abroad does not currently focus on UNSCR 1325 and gender issues specifically, although gender issues are addressed within a package of briefings — operational training and guidance (OPTAG) — aimed at sensitizing military personnel to the particular societies in which they will deploy. MoD wrote that:

> "we have given consideration to how we could strengthen the delivery of our commitment to 1325 and concluded that introducing a mandatory module on 1325 in every OPTAG training would be difficult given the range of issues that have to be covered during the 2–3 weeks of the training."[139]

135. We accept that there are a large number of issues which the MoD must cover with its personnel before deployment but, given the disproportionate effect of conflict on women and girls, discussion of UNSCR 1325 should be a priority. We hope the Government's adoption of an Action Plan to implement UNSCR 1325 will encourage this. In addition, since the MoD invests significant resources in training the military forces of other countries, there should be a greater awareness of UNSCR 1325 throughout the armed forces.

Small arms and light weapons (SALW)

136. The UK Government has committed itself to securing agreement in 2006 to start negotiations on an Arms Trade Treaty (ATT) and to report to the UN General Assembly by 2008. This commitment was reiterated in the DFID White Paper.[140]

---

137 UN SCR 1325 of 31 October 2000. www.un.org

138 Q 68 (Mr Evans, DFID)

139 Ev 118 (DFID)

140 DFID, *Making governance work for the poor*, page 36

137. International concern about the dangers posed by weapons of mass destruction (WMD) has tended to distract from the greater threat to human security posed by the spread of conventional weapons. "There is clear evidence that weak, failing and post-conflict states play a critical role in the global proliferation of small arms and light weapons" as either source, transit or destination country.[141] SALW played a significant part in increasing the duration and intensity of the conflict in Sierra Leone. SALW have also been the main weapons in the wars in Angola, DRC and Sudan.

138. The easy availability of small arms weakens state capacity. DFID addresses the availability of SALW through its security sector reform projects. For example the Global Conflict Prevention Pool's Strategy on Small Arms and Light Weapons has provided around £24 million over the past four years for measures to restrict arms supply, reduce demand and take weapons out of circulation.[142] The UK Government has developed a policy on small arms trade which states that it will not sell arms to known terrorists, or to governments if it believes they will be used to repress the populace. This is, however, often difficult to ascertain in advance. **Weapons stocks frequently end up in the hands of someone other than the original purchaser — as when Siad Barre's weapons stocks in Somalia were distributed among fighting clans in the 1990s. The Ugandan government may appear 'responsible' in relation to its development policy but not necessarily in relation to northern Uganda or the DRC. Arms sales to a government may encourage it to feel immune from criticism by its own people and may also encourage arms acquisition by neighbouring countries. Strong common standards for global trade in conventional weapons should be an international priority. The Government's policy on not selling arms to governments if it believes they will be used to repress the population must be applied robustly.**

139. In response to questioning about the likelihood of agreement on an International Arms Trade Treaty, we were told by Saferworld that:

> "there are a number of obviously pretty important countries which are either overtly opposed to the ATT or have a more subtle approach, but we would assume that they have strong misgivings about an ATT. The challenge to be faced this year is tackling that opposition but also getting the people who have signed up to statements of support to actually be active supporters, pro-active supporters, because the UK Government can lead so far."[143]

140. It is also the case that where, for example, state borders are porous:

> "you have to build up the capacity both of governments to deal with licensing their transfers and monitoring their participation in the regional and international dimension of it, and building up their border controls but also building up their legislation on small arms."[144]

---

141 Stewart Patrick, *Weak States and Global Threats*, *op cit*. footnote 15.

142 Ev 113 (DFID)

143 Q 26 (Claire Hickson, Saferworld)

144 Q 28 (Claire Hickson, Saferworld)

141. **The Government has made good progress in pushing for an International Arms Trade Treaty.**[145] **It must build on this and ensure there is no loss of political momentum on this important issue in the UN. We also draw the Government's attention to the recent Reports which the Quadripartite Committee has published in relation to arms controls. The International Development Committee is both contributor and signatory to those reports and we hope that the Government will take on board the recommendations the Quadripartite Committee makes.**

Regional initiatives – the Africa Peace Facility

142. Those countries and regions affected by conflict are best placed to address peacebuilding and post-conflict reconstruction. Peacebuilding needs to be home-grown, rather than imposed by outsiders. Successful outcomes are most likely to occur where peacebuilding has the support of those affected by the conflict. Because regional organisations operate in close proximity to conflict they have a greater stake in the outcomes and are often much more willing to become involved. In addition, many internal conflicts have significant regional dimensions and, as a consequence, require regional solutions.

143. The New Economic Partnership for Africa (NEPAD) sees peace and security as preconditions for sustainable development. To this end, NEPAD has developed a post-conflict reconstruction policy framework intended to facilitate coherence in the assessment, planning, coordination and monitoring of post-conflict systems. The framework maintains that:

> "external actors should systematically develop the capacity of the internal actors and facilitate the scaling-down of their own role and the scaling-up of the role of the internal actors. Internal actors should be involved in assessment, planning and monitoring processes to the greatest extent possible. As the situation improves the participation of the internal actors should increase until they eventually take full ownership of this function."[146]

144. Many regional organisations, especially in Africa, have limited capacity and resources. Exceptionally, the Economic Community of West African States (ECOWAS) has been quite successful in responding to conflict in the region. The donor community has a responsibility to build up regional organisations to meet the challenges of peacebuilding.

145. In 2004 the EU agreed to finance an African Peace Facility (APF) for three years. The Peace Facility is based on the idea of African ownership — it supports African-led peace-keeping operations as well as capacity-building for the emerging security structure of the AU. Although the APF, currently a £250 million instrument, is mainly funded by the EU, African countries have donated 1.5% of their allocations under the 9th European Development Fund (EDF). They are thus making a significant, if indirect, financial

---

145 See Quadripartite Committee, *Strategic Export Controls, Annual Report for 2004, and Licensing Policy and Parliamentary Scrutiny*, First Joint Report of session 2005-6, HC 873 paras 181-183.

146 NEPAD, African post-conflict reconstruction policy framework, www.nepad.org

contribution. The APF was renewed this year for a further three years, with up to 100 million euros per year over the period 2007–10.[147]

146. The APF has been used to support AU peacekeeping efforts in Darfur. In this respect it is fulfilling the important function of supporting an African-led peacekeeping mission. **In spite of the mismatch between expectations about what the AU can achieve in Darfur, and inadequate institutional capacity and financial resources, the APF has encouraged Africans to step forward as peacekeepers. Given the problems in amassing appropriately sized and effective UN peacekeeping forces, the APF has made a significant contribution to building up an African-led peacekeeping force. We hope that the EU will continue to fund and build up the Africa Peace Facility and urge further such partnerships to strengthen regional capacities. We believe that African governments could and should make substantial additional financial contributions of their own to the AU's peacekeeping forces.**

---

147 Q 199 (Jonas Frederiksen, ECDPM)

5 The Peacebuilding Commission

147. Armed conflict, its threat, and the build-up of arms in many countries has set back development and progress towards the MDGs. If the international community is committed to the achievement of the MDGs the incidence of conflict in developing countries must be addressed directly.

148. The UN system has responded to this phenomenon and the need to address pressing humanitarian issues by launching a number of post-conflict missions known as peacebuilding or peace support operations.[148] The first such operation was in Namibia in 1989. In 2004 the UN Secretary General's High Level Panel proposed the creation of a Peacebuilding Commission and a Peacebuilding Support Office[149] to help states avoid collapse into war and to assist in their transition from war to peace.

149. The Peacebuilding Commission was formally endorsed by the World Summit in September 2005. Its remit is to:

i. Propose integrated strategies for post-conflict peacebuilding and recovery;

ii. Help to ensure predictable financing for early recovery activities and sustained financial investment over the medium-to longer-term;

iii. Extend the period of attention by the international community to post-conflict recovery;

iv. Develop best practices on issues that require extensive collaboration among political, military, humanitarian and development actors.[150]

Absent from the new Commission is a specific preventative mandate, and this lack has been much criticised, in particular by NGOs.[151]

150. The significant difference between the Peacebuilding Commission and previous peacebuilding efforts has been the attempt to move beyond the imposition and observance of a peace agreement and the monitoring of ceasefires toward a much more sustained post-conflict reconstruction effort. Reconstruction, when carried out properly, can provide important incentives for maintaining the peace. We discussed the Peacebuilding Commission in our earlier report on Darfur.[152]

151. The effectiveness of the Peacebuilding Commission will depend on how it interprets its mandate. Concerns have been raised with us that the problem with the Peacebuilding Commission is that the UN as a system operates on the basis of:

---

148 The UN had been involved in peacekeeping before this but this was on a much smaller scale and largely concerned with implementing a peace agreement.

149 UN High Level Panel on Threats, Challenges and Change, *A more secure world: our shared responsibility*, New York: UN 2004

150 www.un.org/peace/peacebuilding

151 Richard Ponzio, *The creation and function of the UN Peacebuilding Commission*, Saferworld, November 2005.

152 Second Report from the International Development Committee, Session 2005-06, *Darfur: The killing continues*, HC 657

> "government to government diplomacy, whereas peacebuilding is not about government to government peacebuilding, it is more about civil society engagement...there is a concern that it will not engage with local communities in the proper way and that needs to be thought about again."[153]

152. Saferworld are concerned that the Peacebuilding Commission should not simply be an office in New York but that it needs to "relate to both UN and donor bodies on the ground but also have an interaction with national authorities and civil society."[154] We agree. The peace which is being built should be one which grows out of the local situation and not one which is imposed by donors or simply reflects the government's interests. Mechanisms should be established to involve civil society so that grievances can be properly addressed in the work of the Peacebuilding Commission.

153. DFID argues that the Peacebuilding Commission's operations should be based on a shared plan between the government of the country it is operating in and the donor community, and that the Peacebuilding Commission must play a key role in reconstruction.[155] **We agree that the operations of the Peacebuilding Commission should be based on a shared plan between the country in question and the donor community but we also consider that excluding civil society organisations runs the risk of downplaying grievances.**

154. The forthcoming DFID policy on conflict due out later this year provides an ideal opportunity for DFID to consolidate its place among development agencies at the forefront of addressing conflict. A DFID conflict policy also has the potential to produce a more coherent, whole-of-government approach to conflict. This report sets out some of the key policy areas and considers ways in which a conflict policy can have a net positive effect on reducing the incidence and recurrence of conflict in developing countries. This in turn would vastly increase the prospects for achieving the Millennium Development Goals, especially in Africa. **While the link between conflict and development is a relatively new field, it is an area to which the Government must give priority in order to improve development outcomes amongst the poorest. Preventing and ending conflicts and helping to ensure they do not recur will do more to create a climate for poverty reduction and development in the countries affected than any amount of costly aid programmes.**

---

153 Q 36 (Oli Brown, IISD)

154 Q 36 (Claire Hickson, Saferworld)

155 DFID, *Making Governance work for the poor*, p 50.

Conclusions and recommendations

1. The idea of human security — linking the spheres of security and development — should form one of the building blocks for policies towards weak and failing states. However, it is important that "northern" security assumptions should not be allowed to distort or undermine efforts to promote security and poverty reduction in Africa in line with DFID's Public Service Agreement and the MDGs. (Paragraph 11)

2. DFID may need to give more thought to the wider 'public relations' impact of the shift away from highly visible support to less visible assistance in post-conflict countries, especially in those where it is the largest bilateral donor. If peace is to be viable, it is important that people perceive both immediate and sustained benefits from it. (Paragraph 15)

3. We accept that the continuing conflict in northern Uganda is not the fault of the Government of Uganda. Nevertheless the Government of Uganda has responsibilities to its population in the north which hitherto it has failed to fulfil. Instead of meeting its responsibilities, the Government of Uganda has been relying on UN agencies to provide core functions such as health and education. This is costing donors US$200 million per year — money which could make a huge development impact if the conflict was resolved and the resources were spent on post-war reconstruction and on resettling displaced people in their villages. (Paragraph 23)

4. The evidence we received in hearings and on our visits leads us to believe that CPCA states are precisely where a large part of development assistance should be focused, and we support DFID in this regard. However, this new approach entails significant risks for DFID — some programmes may not achieve the desired results, others will take much longer than anticipated. DFID cannot work alone in this; it must ensure it has the support of other government departments. The human security approach discussed in Chapter One explicitly demands greater coherence across the whole of Government. (Paragraph 37)

5. We agree with recent changes in HMG's approach to conditionality, away from policy conditionality, but the situation in Sierra Leone demonstrates that DFID can only exert limited leverage on the Government to make the changes needed to reduce corruption, facilitate effective governance and promote development in Sierra Leone. This indicates the importance for DFID teams of prioritising their strategic planning when operating in a post-conflict country — the need constantly to re-evaluate the appropriateness of policies and adjust their operations accordingly. DFID needs to give more thought to the timing and sequencing of the type of aid it employs in countries recently emerged from conflict if it wishes to create more effective states. (Paragraph 41)

6. We recognise that there are difficult policy dilemmas for donors working in countries emerging from conflict, and that 'good enough' government is often a worthwhile achievement. DFID should ensure that it is not excusing wrongful acts as aberrations in an otherwise successful development partnership. (Paragraph 45)

7. Questions about the distribution of humanitarian assistance should be based on need, rather than the particular theoretical stage of a conflict. Such funding should be wound down as needs decrease. ECHO should ensure that key facilities such as the Panzi Hospital are not closed prematurely. Conflict-related services, such as the unit for women victims of sexual violence, will be needed for years to come. Similarly the signing of peace accords should not take international attention and funding away from the process of their implementation. While the cyclical approach is a useful tool, a more integrated approach to the whole of conflict would produce better outcomes. (Paragraph 50)

8. We believe that DFID should pay greater attention to local knowledge and local points of view in their SCA tool. While we recognise that conflict theories can help inform analysis, we would expect DFID to acknowledge the distinctive character of each conflict and to listen to local people. (Paragraph 54)

9. Conflict assessments should be a precondition for engaging in CPCA states and mandatory for all donors. There is no reason why donors should not share the results of such assessments, rather than duplicating efforts. Conflict assessment is a necessary but not a sufficient guarantor of effective development assistance — measures need to be put in place to ensure that the analysis informs policy. The whole of HMG should make use of the analysis resulting from the conflict assessment — it should not be restricted to DFID. In addition, there should be independent evaluations of how well conflict assessments are done. (Paragraph 56)

10. We welcome the continuation of the Conflict Prevention Pools, which are a small but important part of the Government's approach to conflict. They provide an important channel for inter-departmental cooperation in CPCA states, itself a prerequisite for greater effectiveness of HMG actions in difficult environments. However, because the Pools fund relatively small departmental projects they do not by themselves demonstrate a joined-up approach. Policy coherence is desirable but it is important to be clear about the policy around which coherence is sought. (Paragraph 64)

11. We agree that DFID should not commit its resources to "winning hearts and minds", but we understand why it is often necessary for peacekeeping troops to implement quick impact projects to win support from local people. As an exercise in joined-up government, military commanders should consult DFID, and other development agencies, about their proposals for quick impact projects, to try to ensure that they deliver development as well as security benefits. (Paragraph 65)

12. The debate on the eligibility of funding security sector reform through ODA is not going to go away. It is important that the Government monitors and contributes to this debate. The Government will need to take a position on whether or not ODA-eligible expenditure can be extended further. While DFID has a clear policy which seeks to ensure that 90% of its funding goes to the poorest states, and the Pools facilitate expenditure on non-ODA eligible items, other EU members, and the European Commission, do not have such restrictions or the equivalent of the Pools. Given the importance of security sector reform in CPCA states this is a matter of

some urgency. We believe the definition of ODA should not be expanded to include military expenditure. (Paragraph 71)

13. Grievances matter because if they are not properly addressed they risk precipitating a return to conflict. It is a necessary, but not sufficient, step to address only the crimes committed by high level officials and rebel leaders. While this approach, exemplified in the Special Court of Sierra Leone, sends a message of challenging impunity, too often it only scratches the surface. Abuses and crimes carried out at a lower level also need to be addressed in a manner which recognises the impact of the conflict on communities, families and individuals. In this way peacebuilding will have greater local ownership and more chance of lasting. (Paragraph 80)

14. We agree with the ODI that the building up of institutions for democratic accountability should play a larger role in donor governments' support for electoral processes. It would also bring an end to the practice of adopting 'donor darlings' based on personalities rather than conduct and the strength of institutions. This would allow for peaceful transition between rulers and eliminate the perpetuation of one person rule or elites. (Paragraph 87)

15. Institution-building in post-conflict societies is a crucial part of improving governance. Democratic elections are essential for creating a legitimate government. The establishment of a democratic system is a long-term project, which must be owned by the people. Donors should not suppose that one free multi-party election will entrench democracy. Long-term aid will continue to be needed in post-conflict states to build and strengthen accountable institutions and to nurture a democratic culture. (Paragraph 92)

16. We accept that DFID may not be able to place conflict advisers in all conflict settings; consequently the role of regional advisers is even more significant. DFID therefore needs to ensure that regional advisers are visible, and communicating regularly with all branches of the UK Government. (Paragraph 95)

17. Conflicts, the effects of conflict, and the people who wage them, do not always recognize state borders. The building up of trans-national capacities in Africa through the Africa Conflict Prevention Pools is, in our view, the right approach in that it promises to facilitate greater regional ownership of peacebuilding policies. But donors should also give serious consideration to carrying out, if possible jointly, regional conflict analyses as part of their approach to conflict, so that they do not solely succeed in moving problems from one state to the next. (Paragraph 96)

18.   In our view, the Government needs, as a matter of urgency, to take forward the Africa Commission recommendation of a definition of conflict resources, and an Expert Panel in the UN Security Council. Without an agreed definition the international community's approach will continue to be piecemeal, ad hoc and inconsistent. An internationally agreed definition of conflict resources would make it unnecessary to have a 'Kimberley Process' for every resource. (Paragraph 102)

19.   We believe that the Joint Working Group guidelines have contributed to major improvements in the operation of the UK's National Contact Point. (Paragraph 109)

20.   We are surprised and disappointed that the DTI did not contact Afrimex about their activities or investigate the activities of Alfred Knight in relation to the DRC. We believe the DTI could do more to promote the EITI and to resolve issues surrounding conflict resources. (Paragraph 116)

21.   There is a serious deficiency in the manner in which the Government approaches the actions of UK companies abroad, and in particular in CPCA countries. The Government does not send out a strong message to UK companies about the significance it attaches to OECD Guidelines. Given the number of UK companies originally listed by the UN and, given the human rights abuses which we know accompanied the war, and continue to be perpetrated, the Government response should have been more thorough. The Government needs to demonstrate that it takes the OECD guidelines seriously, in practice as well as in theory, by drawing up practical measures to ensure their implementation. (Paragraph 117)

22.   Tools are of little use if they do not change behaviour. The Government has a responsibility to make UK Companies aware of the OECD guidelines and to offer them appropriate advice. There is a pressing need for the UK Government to consider ways to ensure that the approach of the DTI is not at odds with other aspects of Government policy in CPCA states. Without such coherence the Government cannot hope to have the impact it seeks through DFID's new strategy of engagement in fragile states. We intend to take evidence from DTI ministers on these important issues. (Paragraph 119)

23.   We think that the UN Peacekeeping Force in the DRC should be providing some oversight of prison conditions as part of its mandate to "facilitate humanitarian assistance and human rights monitoring, with particular attention to vulnerable groups". It should also consider putting in place effective human rights monitors for prisons. (Paragraph 122)

24.   EU work on the Chain of Payments is an important step in the right direction, but, given the extent of insecurity in the DRC, it is a drop in the ocean. If security sector reform is to be successful in the DRC, a much larger sum of money will need to be found. The newly-elected Government of the DRC will have primary responsibility for this, but it cannot achieve this without outside assistance. Security is the basic precondition for development to take place. In our view, the UK Government needs to press the EU and its member states to make security sector reform a priority. The newly-elected government in the DRC will also need to be encouraged to make this a priority area. (Paragraph 126)

25.   It seems clear that donors in Sierra Leone now need to give priority to employment-generation initiatives, including agricultural schemes, to provide an incentive for rural-urban migrants to return to rural areas. This will mean simultaneously tackling some of the local governance grievances that have led to discontent in rural areas. It may not be appropriate for DFID to engage in this area directly, but as the largest donor in Sierra Leone, the Department ought to provide a lead for other agencies by highlighting the issue and encouraging others to increase their focus on the issue. (Paragraph 129)

26.   Because fragile states are such difficult environments in which to work, donor coordination is particularly important. In the DRC it will be vital for progress. As the largest bilateral donor, the UK Government must continue its efforts at donor harmonisation. We consider that the European Commission is best placed to take the lead on donor coordination in the DRC. (Paragraph 131)

27.   We accept that there are a large number of issues which the MoD must cover with its personnel before deployment but, given the disproportionate effect of conflict on women and girls, discussion of UNSCR 1325 should be a priority. We hope the Government's adoption of an Action Plan to implement UNSCR 1325 will encourage this. In addition, since the MoD invests significant resources in training the military forces of other countries, there should be a greater awareness of UNSCR 1325 throughout the armed forces. (Paragraph 135)

28.   Weapons stocks frequently end up in the hands of someone other than the original purchaser — as when Siad Barre's weapons stocks in Somalia were distributed among fighting clans in the 1990s. The Ugandan government may appear 'responsible' in relation to its development policy but not necessarily in relation to northern Uganda or the DRC. Arms sales to a government may encourage it to feel immune from criticism by its own people and may also encourage arms acquisition by neighbouring countries. Strong common standards for global trade in conventional weapons should be an international priority. The Government's policy on not selling arms to governments if it believes they will be used to repress the population must be applied robustly. (Paragraph 138)

29.   The Government has made good progress in pushing for an International Arms Trade Treaty. It must build on this and ensure there is no loss of political momentum on this important issue in the UN. We also draw the Government's attention to the recent Reports which the Quadripartite Committee have published in relation to arms controls. The International Development Committee is both contributor and signatory to those reports and we hope that the Government will take on board the recommendations the Quadripartite Committee makes. (Paragraph 141)

30.   In spite of the mismatch between expectations about what the AU can achieve in Darfur, and inadequate institutional capacity and financial resources, the APF has encouraged Africans to step forward as peacekeepers. Given the problems in amassing appropriately sized and effective UN peacekeeping forces, the APF has made a significant contribution to building up an African-led peacekeeping force. We hope that the EU will continue to fund and build up the Africa Peace Facility and

urge further such partnerships to strengthen regional capacities. We believe that African governments could and should make substantial additional financial contributions of their own to the AU's peacekeeping forces. (Paragraph 146)

31. We agree that the operations of the Peacebuilding Commission should be based on a shared plan between the country in question and the donor community but we also consider that excluding civil society organisations runs the risk of downplaying grievances. (Paragraph 153)

32. While the link between conflict and development is a relatively new field, it is an area to which the Government must give priority in order to improve development outcomes amongst the poorest. Preventing and ending conflicts and helping to ensure they do not recur will do more to create a climate for poverty reduction and development in the countries affected than any amount of costly aid programmes. (Paragraph 154)

List of acronyms

ACHU	Africa Conflict and Humanitarian Unit
ACPP	Africa Conflict Prevention Pool
APF	African Peace Facility
ARLPI	Acholi Religious Leaders Peace Initiative
ATT	Arms Trade Treaty
CHASE	Conflict, Humanitarian Affairs and Security Department
CPCA	Conflict-prone and conflict-affected
CPIA	Country Policy and Institutional Assessment
CPPs	Conflict Prevention Pools
CSO	Civil Society Organisations
CSR	Corporate Social Responsibility
DAC	OECD Development Assistance Committee
DDR	Demobilisation, disarmament and reintegration
DRC	Democratic Republic of the Congo
ECHO	European Commission Humanitarian Office
ECOWAS	Economic Community of West African States
EDF	European Development Fund
EITI	Extractive Industries Transparency Initiative
EUSEC	The EU's Security Sector Reform Mission in the DRC
FARDC	DRC National Army
FDLR	Forces Démocratique pour la Libération de Rwanda
GCPP	Global Conflict Prevention Pool
ICC	International Criminal Court
ICG	International Crisis Group
IDP	Internally displaced persons
IISD	International Institute for Sustainable Development
IMATT	International Military Advisory and Training Team
JWG	Joint Working Group
LRA	Lord's Resistance Army
MDGs	Millennium Development Goals
MONUC	UN Peacekeeping Force in the DRC
NCP	National Contact Point
NEPAD	New Economic Partnership for Africa
NUAPP	Northern Uganda Advocacy Partnership for Peace
ODA	Official Development Assistance
OECD	Organisation for Economic Cooperation and Development
OPTAG	Operational training and guidance
PRBS	Poverty Reduction Budget Support
PVA	Participatory Vulnerability Analysis
QIP	Quick Impact Projects
RAID	Rights and Accountability in Development
RCD	Rally for Congolese Democracy

SALW	Small arms and light weapons
SCA	Strategic Conflict Assessment
SSR	Security Sector Reform
TRC	Truth and Reconciliation Commission
UN-OCHA	UN Office for the Co-ordination of Humanitarian Affairs
UNSCR	UN Security Council Resolution
WHO	World Health Organisation
WMD	Weapons of Mass Destruction
WTO	World Trade Organisation

Formal minutes

Members present:

Malcolm Bruce, in the Chair

John Barrett	Mr Quentin Davies
John Battle	James Duddridge
Hugh Bayley	Ann McKechin
John Bercow	Joan Ruddock
Richard Burden	Mr Marsha Singh

Draft Report (Conflict and Development: Peacebuilding and Post-conflict Reconstruction), proposed by the Chairman, brought up and read.

Ordered, That the Chairman's draft Report be read a second time, paragraph by paragraph.

Paragraphs 1 to 153 read and agreed to

Summary agreed to.

Resolved, That the Report be the Sixth Report of the Committee to the House.

Ordered, That the Chairman make the Report to the House.

Ordered, That embargoed copies of the Report be made available, in accordance with the provisions of Standing Order No. 134.

Ordered, That the Appendices to the Minutes of Evidence taken before the Committee be reported to the House.

Several papers were ordered to be reported to the House.

[Adjourned till Thursday 19 October at 2.15pm

List of witnesses

List of written evidence

Written evidence submitted by witnesses who also gave oral evidence:

1	Department for International Development	Ev 106, Ev 117, Ev 120
2	ActionAid International	Ev 124; Ev 131
3	Afrimex (UK) Ltd	Ev 133
4	Dr Neil Cooper, University of Bradford	Ev 136
5	Global Witness	Ev 136
6	International Institute for Sustainable Development	Ev 140
7	Professor Robert Picciotto	Ev 145
8	Saferworld	Ev 151

Other written evidence:

9	Sultan Barakat, University of York	Ev 155
10	Center for International Peacebuilding	Ev 159
11	Christian Aid	Ev 163
12	Conciliation Resources	Ev 174
13	Development Workshop Angola	Ev 176
14	International Alert	Ev 179
15	Ministry for Peace	Ev 183
16	Northern Uganda Advocacy Partnership for Peace (NUAPP)	Ev 186
17	One World Action	Ev 192
18	Overseas Development Institute	Ev 199
19	Peaceroots	Ev 202
20	Peace Direct	Ev 204
21	Plan UK	Ev 209
22	Religious Society of Friends (Quakers)	Ev 213
23	Professor Paul Richards	Ev 215
24	Save the Children UK	Ev 216
25	UNDP	Ev 221
26	WOMANKIND Worldwide	Ev 224
27	World Vision	Ev 228
28	Alfred H. Knight Holdings Ltd	Ev 230
29	Krall Métal Congo	Ev 241

List of unprinted written evidence and papers

Additional papers have been received from the following and have been reported to the House but to save printing costs they have not been printed and copies have been placed in the House of Commons Library where they may be inspected by members. Other copies are in the Record Office, House of Lords and are available to the public for inspection. Requests for inspection should be addressed to the Record Office, House of Lords, London SW1. (Tel 020 7219 3074) hours of inspection are from 9:30am to 5:00pm on Mondays to Fridays.

Memoranda

- British Council
- Initiatives of Change, with appendices

Supporting documents submitted with printed memoranda

- Alfred H Knight Holdings Ltd
- Plan UK: transcript and video/DVD: *Children and Young People in Sierra Leone*, January 2006
- Krall Métal Congo

Other background papers

- Correspondence between the International Development Committee and Alfred H Knight International Ltd

Submitted by Afrimex (UK) Ltd:

- UN Security Council: Final report by the Panel of Experts on the Illegal Exploitation of Natural Resources and Other Forms of Wealth of the Democratic Republic of the Congo

Submitted by DFID:

- Background on Crown Agents' Service Package Contract with DFID and the Post Conflict Reconstruction Unit (PCRU)

Submitted by Global Witness and RAID:

- Supplementary papers submitted in advance of the oral evidence session of 4 July 2006

Reports from the International Development Committee

The Government Responses to International Development Committee reports are listed here in brackets by the HC (or Cm) No. after the report they relate to.

Session 2005–06

Printed in the United Kingdom by The Stationery Office Limited
10/2006   350464   19585

ISBN 0-215-03087-7

9 780215 030870